I Believe:
40 Daily Readings
for the Purposeful Presbyterian
The Shape of the Christian Life

Editors
Frank T. Hainer
Mark D. Hinds
Writer
James Adams
Art Director
Jeanne Williams
Cover Design
Rebecca Kueber

Published by Witherspoon Press, a ministry of the General Assembly Council,
Presbyterian Church (U.S.A.), 100 Witherspoon St., Louisville, Kentucky.

PRINTED IN CANADA

www.pcusa.org/witherspoon

I Believe:
40 Daily Readings
for the Purposeful Presbyterian

The Shape of the Christian Life

Introduction v

Theological Disciplines 1
    Day 1 Galatians 3:1–18
    Day 2 Between Doubt and Belief
    Day 3 I Believe What the Church Believes
    Day 4 Can I Do It by Myself?
    Day 5 The Need for Competent Mentors and Allies
    Day 6 To Be an Apprentice Is to Learn a Discipline
    Day 7 The Preservation of the Truth

Disciplines of Love 17
    Day 8 Galatians 5:2–15
    Day 9 Abnormal Behavior
    Day 10 Christian Faith Is Peculiar
    Day 11 Peculiar, but Not Stupid!
    Day 12 Grace and Love
    Day 13 Love Is Something You Do
    Day 14 There's Community in Giving

Disciplining the Flesh 31
    Day 15 Galatians 5:16–26
    Day 16 The "Flesh"
    Day 17 "Flesh" versus Spirit
    Day 18 Naming the Pitfalls
    Day 19 What Can We Rely On?
    Day 20 Can "Church Discipline" Be a Channel of the Spirit?
    Day 21 Personal Disciplines

Spiritual Disciplines 45
    Day 22 Galatians 4:1–7, 12–20
    Day 23 Divisions
    Day 24 Law or Spirit?
    Day 25 Sin Boldly
    Day 26 Crucifying the Flesh
    Day 27 Guided by the Spirit
    Day 28 Specific Disciplines

Disciplines of the Spirit 59
    Day 29 Galatians 6:1–10
    Day 30 Confession or Therapy?
    Day 31 The Need for a Listening Ear
    Day 32 Live and Let Live
    Day 33 Intervention
    Day 34 In a Spirit of Gentleness
    Day 35 Neither Judgmental nor Indifferent

Further Thoughts 71
    Day 36 Discipleship
    Day 37 Ways the Spirit Works
    Day 38 "Lord, Make Us Servants of Your Peace"
    Day 39 Don't Get Tired of Doing the Right Thing
    Day 40 "Give to the Winds Thy Fears"

Small-Group Study Guide 79

Introduction

In the 1970s, there emerged what was, for some, a surprising and even puzzling phenomenon: the so-called "Jesus people." The "Jesus people" of the 1970s bore a certain resemblance to the "flower people" of the 1960s; in fact, many were no doubt the same people. Each group valued simplicity, sharing, inner peace, nonconformity, and passion for a cause. Each group inclined toward certainty. In the community where my family lived, a group of "Jesus people" organized a church. They didn't call it a "church"; they called it a "fellowship." The leaders of the church emerged from the group. Designated by the biblical term "elders," they did not serve for a specified term, but held permanent office. In a very short time, it seemed that the elders had developed extraordinary power. The group did not live together. However, members began to buy homes in the same neighborhood for physical proximity. According to neighborhood conversation, the elders directed the personal affairs of members of the group—even as far as arranging marriages.

Throughout the history of the church, sectarian groups have frequently spun off, concentrating power in the hands of a few leaders. Usually, those who follow such groups are people who have experienced disappointment with the larger church's lack of zeal. They take the gospel seriously, and want it to shape their lives wholly and entirely. If the price is authoritarian rule, they are willing to pay it.

On the other hand, there are Christians who resist any authority at all. Though members of a church, each reserves complete independence in matters of doctrine and morality. They may root antagonism to authority in a vision of the world that sees each individual as absolutely equal. Or, they may root it in a theology that overestimates the capacity of lone individuals to know what is good and to pursue it. Recently, I saw a paid advertisement in a regional newspaper that portrayed the entire history of the church as a history of deception and concentration of power. Having drawn vast oversimplifications, it advocated that people withdraw from their congregations and come together in house churches. Such churches will have no clergy, no officers, no one to tell anyone else what to do.

The examples above portray two extremes. When the accent falls on the authority of officers not accountable to the group, there is danger of tyranny. When the accent falls on the individual as a law unto himself or herself, there is danger of anarchy.

One of the serious religious problems Paul dealt with was the tension between religious tyranny and moral anarchy. He was a Pharisee of the Pharisees, a zealous persecutor of Christians. As a result of his Damascus road experience, Paul turned away from the law as the path to God's acceptance. He turned instead to Christ as the only hope for us. Human inability to fulfill the law is overcome by God in Christ. "God proves his love for us in that while we still were sinners Christ died for us" (*Rom. 5:8*). The question was, having escaped from the tyranny of the law, did the Christian fall into moral anarchy? Freed from the law as the way to please God, was the Christian also free from the obligation to lead a moral life? Absolutely not. And Paul spent a great deal of energy dealing with this concept.

To submit to the teaching authority of the church is to listen carefully to one's own heart, to the word of God in Scripture, and to the many voices that speak to us from their Christian context. It is possible to spend years in formal education without being pushed to think with care and rigor about ultimate things. These readings help us to do just that, as we think along with Paul about the crucial issues of faith, salvation, and the Christian life.

By reading this book, you have embarked on a study of Paul's views of Christian discipleship in the New Testament book of Galatians. The daily readings that follow are designed for individual study and reflection. Perhaps you observe a regular devotional time during your day; these readings could provide content for that important time.

For those who wish to reflect on these readings in a group setting, a small-group study guide is offered on pages 79–106.

Theological Disciplines

You foolish Galatians! Who has bewitched you? It was before your eyes that Jesus Christ was publicly exhibited as crucified! The only thing I want to learn from you is this: Did you receive the Spirit by doing the works of the law or by believing what you heard? Are you so foolish? Having started with the Spirit, are you now ending with the flesh? Did you experience so much for nothing?—if it really was for nothing. Well then, does God supply you with the Spirit and work miracles among you by your doing the works of the law, or by your believing what you heard?

Just as Abraham "believed God, and it was reckoned to him as righteousness," so, you see, those who believe are the descendants of Abraham. And the scripture, foreseeing that God would justify the Gentiles by faith, declared the gospel beforehand to Abraham, saying, "All the Gentiles shall be blessed in you." For this reason, those who believe are blessed with Abraham who believed.

For all who rely on the works of the law are under a curse; for it is written, "Cursed is everyone who does not observe and obey all the things written in the book of the law." Now it is evident that no one is justified before God by the law; for "The one who is righteous will live by faith." But the law does not rest on faith; on the contrary, "Whoever does the works of the law will live by them." Christ redeemed us from the curse of the law by becoming a curse for us—for it is written, "Cursed is everyone who hangs on a tree"—in order that in Christ Jesus the blessing of Abraham might come to the Gentiles, so that we might receive the promise of the Spirit through faith.

Brothers and sisters, I give an example from daily life: once a person's will has been ratified, no one adds to it or annuls it. Now the promises were made to Abraham and to his offspring; it does not say, "And to offsprings," as of many; but it says, "And to your offspring," that is, to one person, who is Christ. My point is this: the law, which came four hundred thirty years later, does not annul a covenant previously ratified by God, so as to nullify the promise. For if the inheritance comes from the law, it no longer comes from the promise; but God granted it to Abraham through the promise.

Between Doubt and Belief

Jesus said, "My kingdom is not of this world. If it were, my servants would fight to prevent my arrest by the Jewish leaders. But now my kingdom is from another place." "You are a king, then!" said Pilate. Jesus answered, "You say that I am a king. In fact, the reason I was born and came into the world is to testify to the truth. Everyone on the side of truth listens to me." "What is truth?" retorted Pilate. With this he went out again to the Jews gathered there and said, "I find no basis for a charge against him."

—John 18:36–38 (TNIV)

Having just conducted a memorial service for a friend and ministerial colleague, I sat at lunch with three others. My wife and I listened as my friend's widow spoke of her husband's hope of eternal life. She reported that in the last days of his life, he had begun speaking of his deceased father, as though he were looking forward to a reunion. Then, referring to the fourth person among us—her close friend—she said, "But you, Ruth, don't really believe in a life after death, do you?" It was a statement rather than a question, and not meant as a judgment. My friend's widow spoke kindly, but Ruth made no reply. It didn't seem the right time for her to express her doubt.

I was grateful that no one asked my opinion. The emotion accompanying the final rites for my friend had left me numb. What felt most real to me was his absence. I could scarcely think about life after death. Yet, a few weeks before, when it appeared that he would die before Easter, I kept thinking that on this Easter he would meet face-to-face the Lord he had proclaimed!

Later in the day, my thoughts kept reverting to this conversation. What did I believe about life after death? I believed in it. I had preached it many times. I had taught the scriptural passages referring to it and affirmed the bold statement of the Apostles' Creed: "I believe . . . in the resurrection of the body; and the life everlasting." I believed, yet I doubted.

Why did I doubt? I doubted because I am part of a society that is immensely skeptical about such things. Though segments of our society seem terribly credulous—believing in angelic interventions, reincarnation, and all sorts of paranormal phenomena—I do not belong to them. I belong to the mainstream of a society that is suspicious of all tradition, but particularly of religious tradition. I belong to the mainstream of a society that is addicted to the belief that science—whether physics, biology, or psychology—has all the answers. That society produces novelists and playwrights and film writers who are suspicious of the church and its gospel. The opinion leaders of secular society believe that when you're dead, you're dead.

Caught between my social environment and my church, I waver between doubt and belief on this matter, even when my faith in Jesus Christ holds firm. So I asked myself what I would have answered if my friend's widow had asked me if I believed in life after death. I would have felt compelled to answer not as a minister—an "authority" speaking officially—but strictly as a friend. Would I speak of my doubt, or put the doubt aside and speak as though possessed of an undisturbed certainty? This is what I decided I would have said: "I believe what the church believes."

Day 3 | I Believe What the Church Believes

What, then, was the purpose of the law? It was added because of transgressions until the Seed to whom the promise referred had come. The law was given through angels and entrusted to a mediator. A mediator, however, implies more than one party; but God is one.
—Galatians 3:19–20 (TNIV)

Wouldn't it be an astonishing abandonment of responsibility to say, "I believe what the church believes"? It would be nothing less than shocking if that statement meant that I grant some institution custody of my conscience! It would be irresponsible if it meant that I yielded permission to the Presbyterian Church (U.S.A.) General Assembly, the pope, or any denomination or council of churches to speak for me. It would be reckless if it meant I surrendered my right and obligation to ask questions or to dissent from official positions. But that's not what I mean when I say, "I believe what the church believes."

What do I mean? I mean that the church is the community I trust most to steer me right. I cannot reach a perfect understanding of the most profound and urgent questions all by myself—not even with the help of an extensive education. I can read the biblical text, but I am not the first one to read it. Others have read before me and pondered it and debated its meaning. Those who write biblical commentaries bring their experience, their scholarship, and lessons from ordinary people to their reading. Even turning for help to a Bible commentary demonstrates how much we rely on an ongoing community of people who read and wrestle with the same texts through the generations.

Many "communities" compete to shape my conscience, my values, and my thinking. Most schools and universities presume a self-contained world with no role for God. While not necessarily hostile to God, learning institutions in our society count it as wisdom to leave matters of faith to the individual. It's quite possible to spend years in formal education without ever being pushed to think with great care and rigor about ultimate things.

The media—and particularly the entertainment media—compete for my attention. Television, film, and novels are more likely to ignore faith or to disdain it than to assist in its formation. Advertising would persuade me that the meaning of life lies in consumption.

Other religious communities—whether the informal New Age variety, new religions such as the Unification Church, or historic religions such as those of the East—command my attention. Various converts with new Arabic names draw attention to the growth of Islam in North America. Movie fans can hardly escape knowing which movie stars belong to the Church of Scientology. In short, the milieu in which I live is not religiously neutral. It consists of diverse communities, each of which makes a bid for my allegiance. That leaves me with an enormous responsibility. Can I sort through all these various religious (and antireligious) options all by myself? Or with a group of friends? Can I hope to acquire enough solid knowledge and intuitive wisdom to find the right path? Certainly I cannot shirk the obligation to search carefully, to question closely, to identify what choices I have to make, and to form a commitment. But am I competent to do that completely independently?

Where do you turn to discover truth?

Do you rely on yourself, perhaps on a gut feeling, or do you seek the counsel of others?

Read John 18:33–38. What is the truth that Jesus is speaking to Pilate?

Can I Do It by Myself?

*Is the law, therefore, opposed to the promises of God? Absolutely not! For
if a law had been given that could impart life, then righteousness would
certainly have come by the law. But Scripture has locked up everything
under the control of sin, so that what was promised, being given through
faith in Jesus Christ, might be given to those who believe.*
—Galatians 3:21–22 (TNIV)

Sometime within the past 250 years, Western society made a
radical departure from traditions of the past. A philosophical
movement called the Enlightenment put an entirely new spin on
the way ordinary people think about themselves. Beginning in the
eighteenth century, people began to see themselves primarily as
individuals. In earlier periods, people saw themselves in their
connectedness with others. People understood themselves as
members of a family, a social class, a professional guild, a religious
community, or a nationality. After the Enlightenment, individuals
sought to distinguish themselves from all such connections. People
did not want to be identified and defined by their belonging, but
by their separate distinctiveness.

This view has a certain merit, of course. By being true to
oneself, a person may develop an identity that is different from—
even at odds with—the values of the family or the group. Just
because my father was a shoemaker, and my grandfather before
him, doesn't mean that I will be my best self as a shoemaker. A
natural artist may be born to a people and community that place
no value on art. One owes it to oneself, to God, and to even the
larger community to discover and develop personal gifts and
independent thinking.

There is value in questioning the way things always have
been. There is value even in looking at cherished ways with a
critical eye. However, as with anything else, one can push
individualism too far. We may very well have reached a point
in North American society in which individualism threatens to
fracture all forms of community.

It's a commonplace view in our society that all people are completely independent in the formation of their own beliefs. Furthermore, no one has the right to question anyone else's beliefs, or even to make judgments of right or wrong, true or false. It's as though our belief in equality of people before God requires us to believe also in an equality of ideas. Is it true that all ideas are equal? All religious beliefs? That everyone is equally right and equally wrong? That there is no truth to be found? Or that, if truth is found, it will be found only one by one?

A young man once said to a pastor in Atlanta, "It's a free country; I can believe what I want to." The pastor replied, "You're right. It's a free country, and you can believe anything you want; but you can't believe the wrong things and have your life turn out right."[1]

1. Aubrey Brown quoting John H. Roark reporting a conversation that included Vernon S. Broyles Jr. of North Avenue Presbyterian Church in Atlanta. *The Presbyterian Outlook*, Vol. 179, No. 18 (May 26, 1997), 8.

Day 5 | The Need for Competent Mentors and Allies

Before the coming of this faith, we were held in custody under the law, locked up until the faith that was to come would be revealed. So the law was put in charge of us until Christ came that we might be justified by faith. Now that this faith has come, we are no longer under the supervision of the law.

—*Galatians 3:23–25 (TNIV)*

"I believe what the church believes" is a way of saying that I have found a community that I trust to guide me in the formation of my faith. I do not surrender my mind or my conscience to that community. I apprentice myself to Jesus Christ, who makes himself known within the community of the church. I hear his voice in its Scripture, its song, its prayer, and its proclamation. I sense his presence in its sacraments, its mission, its pastoral care, and in the voices of brothers and sisters. I commit myself to be Christ's disciple, to learn from him the ways of life and death, and to walk in the hope he sets before me. Yet, I know almost nothing of him except what I know in the church.

The church of which I speak is more than an institution. It's a community of people we describe as "catholic"—meaning, it crosses all cultural and geographic boundaries and erases even the boundaries of time. To this community belong—among countless others—the apostle Paul, John Calvin, Mother Teresa, my spouse, my children, millions of people in Asia and Africa, and the people baptized in our church last Sunday. In this community, I feel I have found both mentors and allies whom I trust. Here exists a community of people—some profound and careful thinkers, some wise from the experience of living—in whose collective faith I have confidence. Is there such a thing as life after death? I have no independent way of knowing whether the answer is yes or no. What I know is that this community—the church of Jesus Christ—has said yes from the beginning, and still says yes. Not that its members are without doubt, for certainly we know the experience of doubt. Even some of our own members, though they are faithful people, do not believe it. But the community as

10

a whole has always believed that, just as God broke the power of death in Jesus' case, God's last word over us is a word of life and not death.

I question, I doubt, I require explanations, but in the end, I trust this community. Everyone, without exception—even the most radical individualist—trusts one "community" more than others. It is this community that carries me when my faith has become too weak to support me. It is in this community that God calls me to support others when my faith is strong and theirs is flagging. In substantial matters of faith, I take responsibility for myself, but do not stand by myself. I believe what the church believes.

$\mathcal{D}$ay 6 | To Be an Apprentice Is to Learn a Discipline

So in Christ Jesus you are all children of God through faith, for all of you who were baptized into Christ have clothed yourselves with Christ. There is neither Jew nor Gentile, neither slave nor free, neither male nor female, for you are all one in Christ Jesus. If you belong to Christ, then you are Abraham's seed, and heirs according to the promise.
—Galatians 3:26–29 (TNIV)

When people feel they have the gift of poetry, how do they develop that gift? I doubt whether a person without such a gift can learn to be a poet. However, a gifted person requires more than an instinct for language and a sensitivity to the emotional environment. To become a poet, one must learn how to use one's natural gifts. That means sitting at the feet of other poets, so to speak, to learn how poetry is created. The gifted person reads the work of other poets, learning the disciplines of poetry and the ways that certain poets have departed from those disciplines or used them unconventionally, but successfully. To become a poet means to apprentice oneself to appropriate mentors and then to find a voice of one's own.

To become a musician or an engineer or an architect or a carpenter involves first apprenticing oneself to those who have already learned how to do it. You may turn out to be a pioneer, breaking new ground—but before you will be a pioneer, you will be an apprentice. It is no small matter to choose your mentors. Choose them carefully, and you will make fewer false starts.

The church is a richly diverse community of North and South Americans, Europeans, Africans, Asians, people long deceased, and people I might reach by phone or by going for a visit. This community—in liturgical language, a "communion of saints"—does not always speak in one voice. Nevertheless, it is within this community that I find my place in an ongoing conversation. Here I find "fathers and brethren"—as the old Presbyterian language used to put it—as well as mothers and sisters. Collectively, this community becomes the mentor necessary for my formation as a Christian. It teaches me the issues and the vocabulary, and passes on to me the experience and serious reflections of the community since the very first generation. Faith itself is a gift of God. To mature in that faith requires acquiring disciplines, just as any kind of maturation does. I choose to learn those disciplines from the people gathered around Jesus Christ. I believe what the church believes.

Day 7 | The Preservation of the Truth

Jesus answered, "I am the way and the truth and the life. No one comes to the Father except through me. If you really know me, you will know my Father as well. From now on, you do know him and have seen him."
—John 14:6–7 (TNIV)

What does all this have to do with the letters of Paul? In his letter to the Galatians, the apostle Paul addressed a conflict in the churches in that region of Asia Minor. Paul had founded the Christian churches in Galatia. Later, preachers approached those congregations with a message drastically different from Paul's. The conflict was theological. Paul had taught that God had invited the Gentiles (non-Jews) to become God's people out of God's overwhelming goodness and generosity. The later preachers argued that Gentiles could not possibly be added to God's people unless they first became Jews. Unless they kept the fundamental rules of the Torah—the laws and the commandments given to the Jewish people—they had no place in God's household. This may seem like an insignificant difference of opinion, but, in fact, it is monumental.

The two sides of the conflict were more like two different religions than variations of the same one. In fact, a council of the church had settled the issue in Jerusalem (*Acts 15*). Notwithstanding, some chose to ignore the consensus reached by the apostles in order to push their own particular agenda. Paul felt quite confident that those who pursue their own way have left the truth behind. He wrote, "I am astonished that you are so quickly deserting the one who called you in the grace of Christ and are turning to a different gospel" (*Gal. 1:6*). He added that the gospel he had preached among the Galatians was "not of human origin . . . but I received it through a revelation of Jesus Christ" (*Gal. 1:11–12*).

Writing to those young churches, Paul rehearsed his own story. He described his early life when he had been zealously anti-Christian. He wrote about his conversion and a subsequent visit with Peter and James, the Lord's brother, in Jerusalem. Paul reported that, on a second visit to Jerusalem, he had checked in with the apostles to be sure that they gave their blessing to his missionary message.

Although the other apostles had given Paul the blessing for which he had asked, apparently Peter (called "Cephas" in Galatians) had wavered under pressure from those who wanted to accommodate the sensitivities of the Jews (*Gal. 2:11–12*). Paul took issue with him publicly. Paul then rehearsed the gospel he preached in Galatia and argued his conviction theologically and by appealing to the Hebrew Scriptures (*Gal. 3:6–18*).

The congregations in Galatia and, finally, the whole church received Paul's letter as representing the gospel they had heard and believed from the beginning. In that way, the letter to the Galatians became a part of the New Testament. The letter is a bold statement that is not afraid to distinguish authentic Christian teaching from false and distorted versions of the gospel propagated by independent preachers.

In accepting Paul's letter as Scripture, the church declared that Paul's gospel of God's generosity (God's grace) is the true and authentic Christian teaching. If we are to keep on course, we must listen with great care to what the church has believed.

NOTES:

Disciplines of Love

Day 8 | Galatians 5:2–15

Listen! I, Paul, am telling you that if you let yourselves be circumcised, Christ will be of no benefit to you. Once again I testify to every man who lets himself be circumcised that he is obliged to obey the entire law. You who want to be justified by the law have cut yourselves off from Christ; you have fallen away from grace. For through the Spirit, by faith, we eagerly wait for the hope of righteousness. For in Christ Jesus neither circumcision nor uncircumcision counts for anything; the only thing that counts is faith working through love.

You were running well; who prevented you from obeying the truth? Such persuasion does not come from the one who calls you. A little yeast leavens the whole batch of dough. I am confident about you in the Lord that you will not think otherwise. But whoever it is that is confusing you will pay the penalty. But my friends, why am I still being persecuted if I am still preaching circumcision? In that case the offense of the cross has been removed. I wish those who unsettle you would castrate themselves!

For you were called to freedom, brothers and sisters; only do not use your freedom as an opportunity for self-indulgence, but through love become slaves to one another. For the whole law is summed up in a single commandment, "You shall love your neighbor as yourself." If, however, you bite and devour one another, take care that you are not consumed by one another.

Abnormal Behavior

> *"The workers who were hired about five in the afternoon came and each received a denarius. So when those came who were hired first, they expected to receive more. But each one of them also received a denarius. When they received it, they began to grumble against the landowner. 'These men who were hired last worked only one hour,' they said, 'and you have made them equal to us who have borne the burden of the work and the heat of the day.' But he answered one of them, 'Friend, I am not being unfair to you. Didn't you agree to work for a denarius? Take your pay and go. I want to give the one who was hired last the same as I gave you. Don't I have the right to do what I want with my own money? Or are you envious because I am generous?' "*
>
> —*Matthew 20:9–15 (TNIV)*

Christian faith calls us to behavior that, by conventional standards, is not "normal." It's normal to believe that "there's no such thing as a free lunch." It's normal to believe that people ought to get exactly what they deserve. It's normal to believe that human beings need to win God over by proving their worthiness. It's normal to think that true religion is keeping the rules—or, at least, not breaking the most important ones—and holding one's neighbor to the same high standard.

In all these expectations, Christian faith is not "normal." On the op-ed page of the March 7, 1997, issue of *The New York Times*, an essay by Judge Albert Tomei describes a family who chose to be something other than "normal."[2] A woman had been sitting through the trial of a man whom a jury found guilty of gunning down her son. Throughout the trial, the defendant showed no sign of remorse. His stare was deadly, a steady "beacon of hate." When the jury announced its verdict of guilty, he didn't turn a hair. At sentencing, the judge offered the victim's mother the opportunity to speak. She looked directly at the man convicted of murdering her son and said, "I could never hate you." When she finished, the victim's grandmother took her turn addressing the defendant. She spoke in biblical language. She said, "You broke

2. Albert Tomei, "Touching the Heart of a Killer," *The New York Times*, March 7, 1997.

the Golden Rule: loving God with all your heart, soul, and mind. You broke the law: loving your neighbor as yourself. I am your neighbor." Then she told him that as she had sat in the courtroom, she had tried to hate him, but failed. "I feel sorry for you because you made a wrong choice."

The words of the dead man's mother and grandmother did what no impassioned speech by the prosecuting attorney could do. The vicious stare, the swagger, and the malicious hatred the killer had projected suddenly melted. The unexpected tenderness of those who had suffered a terrible injury touched a soft, unguarded place within the killer. To have poured out their grief and pain upon the one who had caused it would have been perfectly "normal." His vicious act had brought dreadful suffering upon these women, but they chose not to return evil for evil.

The Christian faith calls us to act in ways that seem counter to the cultural norms. Consider the story recounted by Judge Tomei.

How can you prepare to be such a conduit of God's love and mercy?

Christian Faith Is Peculiar

"So the last will be first, and the first will be last."
—Matthew 20:16 (TNIV)

Christian faith is peculiar because it doesn't square with everyday common sense. Particularly in a society that believes so strongly in free enterprise, an iron logic seems to govern every exchange: You give me something, and I give you something in return. In exchange for a few dollars, you get a Happy Meal. When you invite me for dinner, sooner or later I need to return the invitation. If someone injures me, the law is supposed to punish in proportion to that injury. A kind of ecology—a natural need for balance—calls for us to even everything out in due time. Our economy and our system of justice both proceed from that presupposition. This way of looking at things seems deeply rooted in human nature, not because we are merely products of our society. It would seem as though an inborn sense of justice requires that we pay for everything sooner or later.

Into the churches of Galatia had come preachers governed by this conventional logic. To be a Christian, they said, required first keeping the rule that required the circumcision of every Jewish male. One must be a Jew first, they argued, to be a true Christian. Anyone who failed to meet the minimum ritual requirements could not possibly become a part of God's household.

Apparently, the Galatian Christians had a hard time resisting this way of looking at things. Surely God required something of people before they could claim a place in the household of God! God might require a ritual—why not circumcision, the rite of admission required of all Hebrew males or male converts to Judaism? Paul argued that if anyone thought God's favor could be earned by keeping a ritual, he or she had bought into a false way of thinking. Ritual circumcision was only a small part of God's requirement in the Torah—the holy Law. If people have to prove themselves before being admitted to God's household, they have to keep the whole law—and not just one little part of it.

If they choose that route to try to win God over, they have "cut [themselves] off from Christ" (*Gal. 5:4*). Paul insists that if the Galatians imagine they can give God something to earn admission to God's household, they have "fallen away from grace" (*v. 4*). They have taken the burden of salvation upon themselves. The true gospel teaching, Paul argues, is that God has shouldered the burden of our salvation. We can provide nothing in exchange for God's favor. God has already reached out to us, without having attached any conditions.

This unconditional gift is what the New Testament calls "grace." God reaches out to us by grace—out of a profound love for us that we have not earned and cannot earn. This is what Jesus Christ means, and this is who he is. Christ is God's hand stretched out to us, who cannot pull ourselves up by our own bootstraps. God's heart has opened to us, who could not, by our own methods, pry it open. This departure from the iron law that requires an equal exchange is peculiar.

How is God's justice different from the fair-trade justice that we generally seek?

Peculiar, but Not Stupid!

For in Christ Jesus neither circumcision nor uncircumcision has any value. The only thing that counts is faith expressing itself through love.
—Galatians 5:6 (TNIV)

Christian faith does not operate by conventional logic. If conventional logic led human beings to where we ought to be, we wouldn't need Jesus Christ. The faith that is anchored in Jesus Christ is unconventional but not illogical. It is perfectly reasonable, seen from an insider's point of view.

"Insiders" are simply those who have adjusted their hearts and minds to the new reality disclosed in Christ. On our own, we would not likely reason ourselves into seeing things as Christ teaches us to see them. In fact, there are many critics of Jesus Christ and the way of life into which he leads us. Some do not hesitate to scorn this one who overturns the conventional wisdom. He declares God's love for the single stubborn, lost "sheep" and for the prodigal. He calls us to forgive enemies, to return good for evil, and to serve one another with the same humility as those who bend down to wash the feet of the sojourner.

The church—the community gathered around Jesus Christ—coaches us to see and experience the world in new ways. The church is formed both by Scripture and by the bearer of this treasure from one generation to another. So it is right and proper that the community read Scripture aloud, use the language of Scripture in worship, study it in smaller groups, and sit quietly in the presence of Scripture as the church seeks the mind of Christ.

To doubt, to disbelieve, and to turn one's back on holy things is quite as "natural" as to turn to God in faith. It is "normal" to adopt the conventional wisdom of the societies in which our lives have been rooted. When we become a part of the church, the community patiently coaches us toward new ways of seeing and reasoning. Immersed in Scripture, the church immerses us into a new environment. In that new environment, we experience grace and love in new ways.

You, my brothers and sisters, were called to be free. But do not use your freedom to indulge the sinful nature; rather, serve one another humbly in love.

—Galatians 5:13 (TNIV)

The God of Scripture is a big God! The God known in Scripture is a God who does for us what we cannot do. God reaches out to us, however unworthy, broken, and uncertain we are. God claims us and makes us a part of God's household even though we will never believe quite rightly, behave quite rightly, or trust as fully as we ought.

This is the message of the gospel, embodied in Jesus. The apostle Paul put it in words, and the churches of the Reformation insisted on it in the face of opposition. Our salvation does not rest in our own flawed efforts, but it comes to us as a gift.

The closest parallel, I suppose, is parental love. Parents love their child even when the child is foolish or rebellious. Parents love even the child who causes them the most difficulty and grief. Parents love not because their children have made themselves lovable, but because it is the nature of parents to love. In human situations, there are exceptions. Some parents turn away from their children. In God's case, this persistent love includes all, without exception. The biblical word for such generosity, proceeding from God toward us, is *grace.*

To say that God saves us by grace is to say that salvation is not something we do for ourselves, but something God does for us. This was precisely the issue that caused the apostle Paul to become so angry with the false teachers among the churches of Galatia. To require non-Jews to live by the law of Moses—all of it, or part of it—implied that it is people's responsibility to save themselves. It also implied that such a thing was actually possible. Paul insisted that salvation is a gift and that there is no way in heaven or on earth that human beings might experience salvation except as a gift. "You who want to be justified by the law have cut yourselves off from Christ" (*Gal. 5:4*). Those who attempt self-salvation by rule-keeping have turned away from the God who reaches out to us in Christ.

It's hard for us to believe that God could give us something we need and long for without asking us for something in exchange. Nevertheless, this is precisely what the gospel affirms. Out of pure grace, God invites us to be God's own people. In our own lives, this grace works itself out as love.

Day 13 Love Is Something You Do

For the entire law is fulfilled in keeping this one command: "Love your neighbor as yourself."

—*Galatians 5:14 (TNIV)*

In the letter to the Galatians, Paul reminded these early Christians that the sacred law of the Hebrew people did not bind them. (Neither did the rules or rites of the various Gentile religions bind them.) "For you were called to freedom, brothers and sisters" (*Gal. 5:13*).

Freedom is a wonderful gift to those who have been all tied up in knots worrying about how to keep the rules. When the Iron Curtain fell and the Soviet Union dissolved, many people in Russia felt the intoxicating exhilaration of freedom. However, once the demonstrations were over and the old order had clearly been dismantled, what ought to have happened next? What do you do with your freedom when it's been placed in your hands? You can use it carelessly, self-indulgently, without regard to the interests of anyone else. Or you can use it carefully and responsibly, bearing in mind that your life is interwoven with the lives of others.

Paul, speaking to the Galatians, wrote, ". . . only do not use your freedom as an opportunity for self-indulgence, but through love become slaves to one another" (*Gal. 5:13*). The Greek word translated as "become slaves" is a verb that has the sense of providing loving service. "For the whole law," Paul writes, "is summed up in a single commandment, 'You shall love your neighbor as yourself' " (*Gal. 5:14*).

Those who know God's outreaching generosity have been set free from following precise rules and keeping score of their progress. However, this freedom—so graciously given—turns us graciously toward our neighbor. We have been set free not so that we can turn inward upon ourselves. We have been set free to look out for the interests of our neighbor: "through love become slaves to one another" (*Gal. 5:13*).

But how can we love just because the gospel says we ought to love? We often misunderstand the use of the word *love* in the New Testament. Love is not a feeling—which, after all, people cannot produce out of a sense of obligation. Love is a discipline we undertake out of gratitude to God. Loving actions on our neighbor's behalf—particularly our neighbor in the community of faith—may kindle positive feelings toward the neighbor. But even if it does not, it is possible to behave graciously toward one another. With or without friendly affection, one can seek the best interests of the other. Paul understands the gospel in this way: God's graciousness toward us frees us from excessive anxiety and self-concern, so that we are freed to be gracious to one another.

The same God who sends us to our neighbor also frees brothers and sisters in Christ to look out for us. We are so used to thinking of life in economic terms—"paying our own way"— that we find it hard to accept another's care for us. The gospel insists, despite our uncertainty and even resistance, that God loves us—apart from any question of worthiness. Those with whom we are united in Christ have also been called to love us and serve us— and we grow spiritually when we accept what they offer.

There's Community in Giving

Praise the LORD, all you nations; extol him, all you peoples. For great is his love toward us, and the faithfulness of the LORD endures forever. Praise the LORD.

—*Psalms 117:1–2 (TNIV)*

Maybe your church has had an experience like our congregation has had. We decided to build a house as one of twenty to be constructed in a weeklong "Blitz Build" under the auspices of Habitat for Humanity. This required that we raise a good deal of money over and above the regular budget. It also required that we recruit many volunteers—some skilled enough to help guide the work of the unskilled. The money came in slowly over a period of months. Then, in the last couple of weeks, it began to come in more rapidly, until we reached the goal and then surpassed it. Volunteers came out of the woodwork to offer their labor. We spent one of the hottest weeks of the summer building the house, and then turned it over to its new owner—a single mother with three children.

The new owner of the house is our "neighbor," by biblical definition. Did we love her? The truth is that none of us had any notion who the owner would be until we had already raised the money and had begun work on the house. As she worked alongside us, many developed an affection for her and for the children we did not know.

Nevertheless, what our congregation did was not based on any particular feeling toward a specific person. Yet it was certainly loving in the biblical understanding of love. We felt called to do something gracious for our neighbor—to seek her best interests. In the process, we rediscovered one another and some of the delights of being part of the community of God's people.

If your congregation has worked on such a project, you know how remarkably the money and the labor seem to materialize. Why is that? Is it because people feel obligated to do a good deed? Because they imagine that they will earn credit in heaven for it?

It's hard to be sure about motives. Still, I don't think that there is a sense of obligation, or a sense of piling up credit with God. I think that people who have experienced some kind of grace in their lives have grace left over for someone else. We give of ourselves not because we have to, but because God's graciousness somehow overflows in and through us. What is strange is that, in our giving, we find ourselves feeling that we end up with more rather than with less.

God's love doesn't run out!

Building a Habitat house or supporting the work of the church with finances, time, and energy should not be construed as "paying off" God. God's invitation to be a part of the household of God is purely gracious—unconditional. However, God's kindness toward us produces an effect when we recognize and actively welcome that kindness. The apostle wrote to the Galatians, "For in Christ Jesus neither circumcision nor uncircumcision counts for anything; the only thing that counts is faith working through love" (*Gal. 5:6*).

Faith is more than simply believing that there is a God. Faith is confidence in God and in God's promises. In faith, we receive the gifts God puts in our hands. The gifts are ours anyway, whether we welcome them or not. When we claim them, they begin to transform the way we see and experience ourselves in the world. Something of God's unconditional generosity begins to be manifest in us. Our "normal" insecurity—fear of loss—begins to lose its grip on us, and we find ourselves being released to give ourselves to our neighbors. "The only thing that counts," then, "is faith working through love."

Christian faith may not be "normal" by the standards of society, but wherever it takes hold, God's incredible generosity makes itself known in lives that slowly conform themselves to a new way of reasoning.

NOTES:

Disciplining the Flesh

Live by the Spirit, I say, and do not gratify the desires of the flesh. For what the flesh desires is opposed to the Spirit, and what the Spirit desires is opposed to the flesh; for these are opposed to each other, to prevent you from doing what you want. But if you are led by the Spirit, you are not subject to the law. Now the works of the flesh are obvious: fornication, impurity, licentiousness, idolatry, sorcery, enmities, strife, jealousy, anger, quarrels, dissensions, factions, envy, drunkenness, carousing, and things like these. I am warning you, as I warned you before: those who do such things will not inherit the kingdom of God.

By contrast, the fruit of the Spirit is love, joy, peace, patience, kindness, generosity, faithfulness, gentleness, and self-control. There is no law against such things. And those who belong to Christ Jesus have crucified the flesh with its passions and desires. If we live by the Spirit, let us also be guided by the Spirit. Let us not become conceited, competing against one another, envying one another.

The "Flesh"

Meanwhile, Saul was still breathing out murderous threats against the Lord's disciples. He went to the high priest and asked him for letters to the synagogues in Damascus, so that if he found any there who belonged to the Way, whether men or women, he might take them as prisoners to Jerusalem. As he neared Damascus on his journey, suddenly a light from heaven flashed around him. He fell to the ground and heard a voice say to him, "Saul, Saul, why do you persecute me?" "Who are you, Lord?" Saul asked. "I am Jesus, whom you are persecuting," he replied. "Now get up and go into the city, and you will be told what you must do."
—*Acts 9:1–6 (TNIV)*

Recently I heard a radio interview with a scholar whose theme was the relation between monotheism and violence. She had, of course, discovered in the Hebrew Scriptures a good many episodes of individual and group violence, jealousy, and dysfunctional behavior. She expressed a wistful regret that the Scriptures did not offer a better example of human beings getting along with one another.

Her reflections caused me to wonder what kind of Bible that might be. If there were no anger in the Bible—no violence, no lust for revenge, no broken relationships, no cruelty—would I be able to find myself there? Would I recognize my world in the world of the Bible? Would I be tempted to believe that somewhere people of faith don't have to struggle against self-centeredness, cruelty, and violence in themselves and their communities? If there were a Bible like that, it would be so distant from reality that it would have lost its appeal to honest people centuries ago. In fact, what makes the Scriptures useful is that they never forget that even the best human beings are torn by forces they do not entirely understand.

In his letter to the churches of Galatia, Paul warned against gratifying "the desires of the flesh" (*Gal. 5:16*). When Paul speaks of "the flesh," he uses a Greek word that does not refer exclusively to the physical body or its impulses. He uses the word more broadly to mean "human nature." Along with the other biblical writers, Paul takes a realistic view of human beings. Human beings know, for the most part, what things are good, useful, and likely to contribute to our well-being. Nevertheless, we find ourselves driven by forces we cannot precisely identify or understand. When we lose the struggle against those forces, as we often do, we descend into antisocial and self-defeating behavior. The struggle to live up to our own most beautiful visions is a struggle against the shadowy part of our own nature. Paul's shorthand for that shadowy part is "the flesh."

Our society exploits human weakness. The genius of the free-market economic system is that, rather than appealing to abstract idealism, it appeals to our longings. Pornography is a dramatic example, but subtler methods exist that appeal to our longings. Advertising suggests that something might be wrong with us if our teeth are less than perfectly white, if our shape doesn't fit the ideal for men or women, or if we haven't cultivated an appetite for certain kinds of food, drink, clothing, or cars that exhibit both our sophistication and our prosperity. Other less direct messages press on us relentlessly, suggesting that this latest technology or that piece of jewelry will reduce our sense of incompleteness or imperfection. The judicious consumer knows better, but each of us has some weakness that makes us vulnerable to just the right temptation. Our society relies heavily on the suggestion that disciplined sexuality, for example, is a hang-up—the sign of a repressed, immature personality. Sexual suggestion not only sells products, but also conspires continually to make us believe that we are doomed to live a disappointing life if we resist temptation.

The apostle wrote about this struggle out of his own experience. In his letter to the Romans, he had written, "For I do not do the good I want, but the evil I do not want is what I do" (*Rom. 7:19*). Surely we can all identify with Paul's experience. We know what is right and have often resolved to live by what we know. Nevertheless, in a crucial moment of severe temptation, we manage to justify seizing that very thing we had intended to refuse.

"Flesh" versus Spirit

I want you to know, brothers and sisters, that the gospel I preached is not of human origin. I did not receive it from any human source, nor was I taught it; rather, I received it by revelation from Jesus Christ. For you have heard of my previous way of life in Judaism, how intensely I persecuted the church of God and tried to destroy it. I was advancing in Judaism beyond many of my own age among my people and was extremely zealous for the traditions of my fathers. But when God, who set me apart from birth and called me by his grace, was pleased to reveal his Son in me so that I might preach him among the Gentiles, my immediate response was not to consult any human being. I did not go up to Jerusalem to see those who were apostles before I was, but I went into Arabia. Later I returned to Damascus. Then after three years, I went up to Jerusalem to get acquainted with Cephas and stayed with him fifteen days. I saw none of the other apostles—only James, the Lord's brother. I assure you before God that what I am writing you is no lie. Then I went to Syria and Cilicia. I was personally unknown to the churches of Judea that are in Christ. They only heard the report: "The man who formerly persecuted us is now preaching the faith he once tried to destroy." And they praised God because of me.

—Galatians 1:11–24

Paul exhorted the Christians of Galatia when he said: "Live by the Spirit . . . and do not gratify the desires of the flesh" (*Gal. 5:16*). It may not be immediately obvious that he is continuing the same argument made earlier in his letter. The false preachers who had come into the Galatian churches had been trying to persuade the people of those congregations that they needed to become Jews before they truly could be Christians. At the very least, the preachers said, males needed to observe the rite of circumcision. Paul had fiercely opposed these preachers, arguing that every man who allowed himself to be circumcised was "obliged to obey the entire law" (*Gal. 5:3*). He insisted that there was no salvation in keeping the law of Moses—whatever merit it might have. To choose to live by the law was a choice one made to try to bargain with God. In effect, those who made that choice had cut themselves off from their only means of salvation—God's mercy extended in Christ. Paul argues that "if you are led by the Spirit, you are not subject to the law" (*Gal. 5:18*).

In other words, the apostle had called Christians to trust radically in God's generosity, offered unconditionally in Christ. To "live by the Spirit" is to live by grace. Whoever lives by the Spirit refuses to indulge a false confidence that anyone can be successful in pleasing God by a scrupulous keeping of the law. Instead, such people rest their entire confidence in Jesus Christ.

It may seem as though living by the Spirit means to live without any sort of restraint. Not so! To live by the Spirit rather than the flesh is to look for and trust God's help in overcoming the impulses that drive us away from God and one another. It is a "third way"—neither enslavement to the rules nor a reckless freedom that ignores or defies the rules. It takes seriously resisting temptation and doing the right thing, just as those who devote themselves to rule keeping take rules seriously. However, it relies on a different remedy. Rather than placing one's hope in one's own determination to do the right thing, it casts all hope upon God's supporting power—the Holy Spirit.

Now the works of the flesh are obvious: fornication, impurity, licentiousness, idolatry, sorcery, enmities, strife, jealousy, anger, quarrels, dissensions, factions, envy, drunkenness, carousing, and things like these. I am warning you, as I warned you before: those who do such things will not inherit the kingdom of God.

—Galatians 5:19–21

The apostle Paul proceeds to name what he calls "the works of the flesh"—in other words, those things that, appealing to our baser nature, threaten to seduce us. It's not clear whether Paul intended to make a comprehensive list. He tells us that the behaviors he names as being "of the flesh" are "obvious."

He lists sexual misbehavior first: fornication, impurity, and licentiousness. Two specifically "religious" violations follow: idolatry and sorcery. Then he names behaviors that disrupt human relationships: enmities, strife, jealousy, anger, quarrels, dissensions, factions, and envy. Finally, he closes with two words describing behavior that lacks self-control and leads to scandal: drunkenness and carousing. In case he has missed anything, he adds "and things like these" (*Gal. 5:19–21*).

All the misbehaviors Paul named separate us from our best selves, from God, and from one another. However we may seek to excuse them, they have a caustic effect on us and all our relationships. As though to hoist a sign with a skull and crossbones on it, Paul adds a fierce postscript: "I am warning you, as I warned you before: those who do such things will not inherit the kingdom of God" (*Gal. 5:21*).

This dire warning would seem to put us in a hopeless situation. It would also seem that Paul is backpedaling from the argument he has been making throughout this letter. Isn't he suggesting that we determine our eternal destiny by avoiding the pitfalls he has named?

How is that different from earning one's own salvation by keeping the announced rules? As Paul clearly understands it, living by the Spirit is in no way a license to discard the obligation to live a moral life. The obligation remains; it is undiminished. In fact, Paul believes in living a moral life as earnestly as he did when, before his conversion, he was a zealous keeper of the law.

The difference is that those who live by the Spirit live moral lives out of gratitude for the astonishing generosity of God—the very God who calls us to be members of the household of God for no reason except God's love for us. Those who live by grace rather than by law do so out of thanksgiving rather than out of a duty to prove themselves worthy. The Christian earnestly seeks the moral life. In this search, Christians rely on something different—presumably more effective—than an impersonal code of law. It is a personal relationship—not a written code—that empowers a moral life.

Explore the connection between the list of good qualities in Galatians 5:22–23 and the law that Paul is so upset about in the earlier portions of this letter.

How might the list lead the people back to following the letter of the law?

How might it help them avoid that?

What Can We Rely On?

By contrast, the fruit of the Spirit is love, joy, peace, patience, kindness, generosity, faithfulness, gentleness, and self-control. There is no law against such things. And those who belong to Christ Jesus have crucified the flesh with its passions and desires. If we live by the Spirit, let us also be guided by the Spirit. Let us not become conceited, competing against one another, envying one another.

—Galatians 5:22–26

What does it mean to live by the Spirit—to trust entirely in Jesus Christ? To live a moral life based on a loving relationship with God rather than a fixed and impersonal set of rules? If the rules aren't enough to restrain us from destructive behaviors, how can the Spirit help us? If "flesh" and "Spirit" are opposed to one another (*Gal. 5:17*), how can we, knowing ourselves as we do, entertain any hope that the Spirit will prevail in our lives?

It seems to have become commonplace in our culture: a respected pastor or priest with a dynamic ministry confesses to misbehavior, often of a sexual or financial nature. Suspicions and allegations of immoral, unethical, or illegal behavior by hypocritical religious leaders feed the voracious appetite of the news media. Ministers, like all people who exert a measure of power and influence, are susceptible to the particular temptations power affords.

Certainly there is no denying that sexual temptation is powerful, particularly in a sexually charged society such as our own. The potential pitfalls are obvious. How might a pastor—or any Christian—avoid those pitfalls with the help of the Spirit? Apart from personal disciplines (to be discussed later), are there communal disciplines that might help? In highly structured denominations, such as the Presbyterian Church (U.S.A.), many safeguards serve to discourage misbehavior by ministers. Where ecclesiastical bodies are charged with oversight of churches and ministers, ministers will be aware that others are concerned about their behavior. While there are no guarantees, such oversight frequently serves to heighten consciousness of one's moral responsibilities.

Where ecclesiastical bodies provide some sort of nurture—particularly for ministers in crisis or under stress—there may be a sense of support that can restrain impulsive behavior. In other words, the Spirit can work through the oversight and mutual admonitions of the church. The community of faith provides a milieu that supports those ministers who, in good faith, look for some tangible expression of the Spirit's presence and power to strengthen them.

Can "Church Discipline" Be a Channel of the Spirit?

Then Jesus said to the crowds and to his disciples: "The teachers of the law and the Pharisees sit in Moses' seat. So you must be careful to do everything they tell you. But do not do what they do, for they do not practice what they preach. They tie up heavy, cumbersome loads and put them on other people's shoulders, but they themselves are not willing to lift a finger to move them. Everything they do is done for people to see: They make their phylacteries wide and the tassels on their garments long; they love the place of honor at banquets and the most important seats in the synagogues; they love to be greeted with respect in the marketplaces and to have people call them 'Rabbi.' But you are not to be called 'Rabbi,' for you have only one Master and you are all brothers. And do not call anyone on earth 'father,' for you have one Father, and he is in heaven. Nor are you to be called 'teacher,' for you have one Teacher, the Messiah. The greatest among you will be your servant. For those who exalt themselves will be humbled, and those who humble themselves will be exalted."

—*Matthew 23:1–12 (TNIV)*

Q. 85. How is the kingdom of heaven shut and opened by Christian discipline?

A. In this way: Christ commanded that those who bear the Christian name in an unchristian way either in doctrine or in life should be given brotherly admonition. If they do not give up their errors or evil ways, notification is given to the church or to those ordained for this by the church. Then, if they do not change after this warning, they are forbidden to partake of the holy Sacraments and are thus excluded from the communion of the church and by God himself from the kingdom of Christ. However, if they promise and show real amendment, they are received again as members of Christ and of the church.

—The Heidelberg Catechism

Once upon a time, in Presbyterian denominations, the church provided oversight for lay members. In varying degrees, church sessions 125 years ago took responsibility for watching over the members of their congregation. If members of the church engaged in some form of notorious behavior, the session would likely require them to appear before the elders. The session would warn against destructive or scandalous behavior. The session could, if a member refused to alter his or her course, cut that person off from the Lord's Table, or even from church membership.

Clearly, with such power vested in the church elders, opportunity was abundant for the abuse of power. Nevertheless, church members valued their membership in the church, cherished their access to the Lord's Table, and no doubt frequently profited by knowing that their church took an interest in their success in living the Christian life. Might it not be that the Spirit was at work through the organs of the church to strengthen members in their resolve to live as heirs of a gracious God?

The church's oversight of its ministers (and sometimes its elders) seems to show that the community can be involved in mediating the Spirit in ways that are more helpful than oppressive. Still, the ways that were familiar to people in the nineteenth century too closely resemble a courtroom. Is there some way that the church as a community of faith could engage in mutual admonition and support in a positive and nonthreatening way? I think there are such ways, but they are likely to be effective only with those who resort to them voluntarily. The Spirit may be mediated to church members in the course of pastoral care. The Spirit may be mediated to members through the exchanges that are part of a small group studying Scripture, praying together, discussing theological or ethical issues, or simply sharing their lives with one another. Each seeks wisdom from the community represented in the group. Is it possible that there are other non-oppressive ways that church officers might learn how to take their rightful responsibility "to tend the flock of God" (*1 Pet. 5:2*)?

Personal Disciplines

Rejoice in hope, be patient in suffering, persevere in prayer.
—Romans 12:12

If Christian morality flows out of a thankful relationship with a gracious God, then the first step is to look continually for ways to deepen that relationship. One way to grow in our relationship with God is through daily prayer, alone or with others. Most often we think of prayer as a catalog of "wants" that we lay before God. Nothing is wrong with bringing our needs or our wants before God—uncensored and without self-consciousness—just as children feel free to run to a parent. In fact, opening our inner life to God will certainly require exposing our needs and longings. Like a wise parent, God can sort it all out and respond out of God's wisdom.

Prayer, however, is more than simply pouring out our yearnings. Prayer may take the form of praise, not because God needs or requires it, but because the offering of praise meets some inner need of ours to give it. Prayer may take the form of words—our own or a phrase from Scripture—or be expressed in hymn, song, or chant. Prayer may be an expectant silence in the presence of God. In that silence, God may offer a word of direction. On the other hand, the silence may be enough in itself. In silence, we sit in the presence of God, not insisting that God provide an answer or spell out a "game plan." Whatever form it takes, prayer is a way of building a friendship with God. That friendship is a means by which the Spirit empowers us to live a grace-filled life.

It is said that Martin Luther, oppressed by a sense of doubt, rebuked the tormenting demons and cried aloud, "I am baptized!" The ancient baptismal rite—and some new ones as well—include explicit renunciations of "the ways of sin" as well as "evil and its power in the world."[3]

3. *Book of Common Worship* (Louisville: Westminster/John Knox Press, 1993), 407.

In the congregation I serve there are at least two opportunities every year to renew one's baptism. One is on the Sunday following Epiphany called the "Baptism of the Lord." The other is on the Saturday evening before Easter Sunday. In renewal of baptism, we lay claim once again to the promise made in our baptism—that is, that God has claimed us, promised to be our God, and freed us from sin and death. Whenever we reclaim our baptismal promises, we follow in the footsteps of Luther, defiantly rebuking the tempter by raising the shield of God's utterly faithful promise. Out of gratitude, then, rather than slavish obligation, we commit ourselves to resisting temptation and walking in the way of the Lord.

Spiritual Disciplines

My point is this: heirs, as long as they are minors, are no better than slaves, though they are the owners of all the property; but they remain under guardians and trustees until the date set by the father. So with us; while we were minors, we were enslaved to the elemental spirits of the world. But when the fullness of time had come, God sent his Son, born of a woman, born under the law, in order to redeem those who were under the law, so that we might receive adoption as children. And because you are children, God has sent the Spirit of his Son into our hearts, crying, "Abba! Father!" So you are no longer a slave but a child, and if a child then also an heir, through God.

Friends, I beg you, become as I am, for I also have become as you are. You have done me no wrong. You know that it was because of a physical infirmity that I first announced the gospel to you; though my condition put you to the test, you did not scorn or despise me, but welcomed me as an angel of God, as Christ Jesus. What has become of the goodwill you felt? For I testify that, had it been possible, you would have torn out your eyes and given them to me. Have I now become your enemy by telling you the truth? They make much of you, but for no good purpose; they want to exclude you, so that you may make much of them. It is good to be made much of for a good purpose at all times, and not only when I am present with you. My little children, for whom I am again in the pain of childbirth until Christ is formed in you, I wish I were present with you now and could change my tone, for I am perplexed about you.

For you were called to freedom, brothers and sisters; only do not use your freedom as an opportunity for self-indulgence, but through love become slaves to one another. For the whole law is summed up in a single commandment, "You shall love your neighbor as yourself." If, however, you bite and devour one another, take care that you are not consumed by one another.

—*Galatians 5:13–15*

The tensions the Galatians experienced are not so very different from tensions well known to people who work in the church today. In today's church, there are those who understand the Christian gospel to be a kind of new law. They look to the text of Scripture to identify specific behaviors that are forbidden or required. The New Testament's message of freedom from the law strikes others so forcefully that it moves them to leave matters of behavior entirely to private judgment.

Identifying groups within the church in terms of such sharp contrasts may not be fair. In fact, few would admit to either extreme. Nevertheless, these tendencies are very much at work among Christians today. It seems as though the great issues that have divided opinion most sharply in the church since the 1960s center on sexuality. In particular, people of good conscience have taken quite different positions on the question of homosexuality. For some, the question of the moral status of homosexual practice is quite simple. After all, in both Old and New Testaments one can find explicit condemnations of sexual activity between people of the same sex. The rule is stated. It is a biblical rule. Therefore, it is a sacrosanct religious law that any devout person must recognize and keep.

At the opposite end of the spectrum are those who believe that Christian freedom releases us from any specific rules of moral behavior. A number of years ago, a major denomination rejected a document that proposed new ways of thinking about human sexuality. Instead of ruling out any particular sexual behaviors, the document suggested that people evaluate any potential sexual situation using the criteria of "love and justice." In other words, rather than presuming that adultery or homosexual relationships are always forbidden, one must consider whether any particular sexual relationship is loving and just.

There is a certain logic to using this measurement of morality. After all, if a relationship is loving and just, how can it be an offense before God? The problem lies in trying to use this way of measuring morality in a specific situation. Who is to say whether a potential sexual relationship is loving or just? Is this a question for those actually considering entering a relationship? If so, can they be trusted to make an unbiased judgment?

Assessing whether a potential relationship is loving and just is incredibly complicated when the assessment is sensitive to the interests of all conceivable parties. Having to decide what is loving and just also seems to presume that the human beings trying to decide are not sinners—in other words, that they are not vulnerable to temptation, rationalization, and self-justification. It may be literally true to declare that sexual relationships that are loving and just are by definition moral. However, it is of no practical use to recommend measuring specific behaviors by these imprecise terms. Those in the heat of passion are the least likely people to correctly judge whether their behavior is either just or loving. The claim that one's sexual behavior satisfies that standard of measurement may offer a mere appearance of morality. There is a strong likelihood, in fact, that we shall deceive ourselves.

Law or Spirit?

For God has done what the law, weakened by the flesh, could not do: by
sending his own Son in the likeness of sinful flesh, and to deal with sin,
he condemned sin in the flesh, so that the just requirement of the law
might be fulfilled in us, who walk not according to the flesh but
according to the Spirit. For those who live according to he flesh set their
minds on the things of the flesh, but those who live according to the
Spirit set their minds on the things of the Spirit.

—Romans 8:3–5

The apostle Paul's experience persuaded him that whoever chose
to approach God by keeping the religious law had chosen a sure
path to failure. It was not that the law did not tell the truth about
what God desires of human beings. It was that no human being
could possibly keep the law well enough. The law shows us what
we ought to be and do and keeps track of where we have failed. In
Christ, God has directed us away from the futility of law keeping
and has created a new way, which is grounded in God's mercy
rather than in our talent at following rules. God's mercy takes the
form not only of forgiveness, but also of active help and support in
living a godly life. That gracious help is the gift of the Holy Spirit.

In his letter to the confused Galatians, Paul urged them to
"live by the Spirit." Nevertheless, he did not hesitate to list certain
kinds of behavior to avoid. (See *Gal. 5:19–21.*) Likewise, Paul felt
confident in describing in rather precise terms what he called "the
fruit of the Spirit." In other words, those who trust the Spirit to
form them in the image of Christ (*Gal. 4:19*) will exhibit traits that
look like these: "love, joy, peace, patience, kindness, generosity,
faithfulness, gentleness, and self-control" (*Gal. 5:22–23*).

It is puzzling that, while Paul cautions against rule keeping,
he does not hesitate to identify particular qualities of character
that ought to be taking shape in the believer. So what do we have
here? A new rule, spelled out as a list of forbidden behaviors and
positive spiritual attributes? Has Paul merely substituted his own
law for the Torah law? Paul would certainly deny that any rule—
complex or simple, God's rule or Paul's—has the power to save us

from ourselves. He is not stating a new basic law, but rather he is describing the way he believes the Spirit will become manifest in the lives of Christians. The Spirit, after all, is not hostile to the old commandments, which indeed displayed quite accurately the ideal way to live. Those who live by the Spirit rather than by the law are not freed to adopt a new morality. Instead, they have been set free to live godly lives without anxious score keeping, trusting that their entire hope rests in God rather than in their own moral successes. Therefore, Paul feels no embarrassment when he describes what a healthy spiritual life looks like. He does not set down rules to be kept, but paints a picture of life lived by the Spirit. Such a life is not less moral, but is at least as vigorously moral as that advocated in the now-obsolete law.

Sin Boldly

There is therefore now no condemnation for those who are in Christ Jesus. For the law of the Spirit of life in Christ Jesus has set you free from the law of sin and of death. For God has done what the law, weakened by the flesh, could not do: by sending his own Son in the likeness of sinful flesh, and to deal with sin, he condemned sin in the flesh, so that the just requirement of the law might be fulfilled in us, who walk not according to the flesh but according to the Spirit.

—Romans 8:1–4

Martin Luther became part of what came to be known as the Protestant Reformation when he made a life-changing discovery. Reading Scripture, Luther was startled by Paul's message with its clarity: God saves us out of a generous mercy—by grace. There was no salvation in following prescribed rules—whether Hebrew Torah or medieval church rules. It was quite clear to Luther that those saved by grace had been called, out of sheer gratitude, to live a grace-filled life. It was also quite clear to him that not even the saintliest Christian would make a complete success of that. In one of his writings, Luther suggested that, because Christians would always fall short of the mark, they ought to "sin boldly."

Luther did not mean that believers should be complacent about their moral failures. He meant that they should not be paralyzed by the likelihood of failure. Rather than live with excessive caution, they should make their best judgments and live boldly, confident that God's mercy will cover their mistakes. It is better to risk being wrong than to live fearful, anxious lives. Better to commit a sin than to hide from God!

I believe Paul would have appreciated Luther's point of view. Paul did not hesitate to describe the shape of a Christian life. Yet he could not possibly predict precisely how that shape would imprint itself on every conceivable situation. Paul himself was bold—not only in his far-ranging missionary travels, but in expressing with almost embarrassing certainty the meaning of the gospel he had received.

Responsible people of conscience in the church clearly do not agree precisely on what sorts of sexual behavior, for example, are compatible with Christian faith and life. Certainly they agree on the basic shape of that life. It should be one noted for love, joy, peace, patience, kindness, generosity, faithfulness, gentleness, and self-control. Where believers of good conscience cannot reach a consensus, perhaps they may grant each other permission to press on boldly nevertheless. It is, after all, God's grace that saves us and not our getting everything exactly right. A good and glad thing, since none of us will ever get everything "exactly right"!

> *Live by the Spirit, I say, and do not gratify the desires of the flesh. For what the flesh desires is opposed to the Spirit, and what the Spirit desires is opposed to the flesh; for these are opposed to each other, to prevent you from doing what you want.*
>
> *—Galatians 5:16–17*

Is it possible that the "fruit of the Spirit" may look different in various contexts? In other words, might the "fruit of the Spirit" manifest itself somewhat differently among urban dwellers than in small, rural communities? Is it possible that the "fruit of the Spirit" may have a somewhat different taste and texture among lay people in the early years of the twenty-first century than in a twelfth-century monastic community? Is it conceivable that the "fruit of the Spirit" might exhibit itself a little differently in a crowded society concerned about population explosions and accompanying environmental threats, where women and men postpone marriage until their twenties or thirties? Certainly love, joy, peace, patience, and so forth will always be recognizable in any century or any cultural setting. Nevertheless, it's possible that they may work themselves out in ways that only the context makes understandable.

Paul makes a strange statement. It may describe what does not change while Christians manifest "the fruit of the Spirit" in different places, times, and social contexts. He wrote to the Galatians that "those who belong to Christ Jesus have crucified the flesh with its passions and desires" (*Gal. 5:24*). This has a strange sound to us. It sounds almost monastic—as though the ideal Christian life might be to deny the very human appetites common to us all. Is Paul calling Christians to a life of asceticism? Is Christian faith, as he understands it, suspicious of the body and its needs? Is he calling us to cold showers, hair shirts, and self-administered whippings to keep our thoughts from straying in dangerous directions? It may be, in fact, that Paul felt an extraordinary concern that Christians tame their sexual appetites. The sexual drive is intensely powerful, and it not infrequently enslaves people who cannot manage it. Sexual misbehavior can be disruptive to the lives of spouses, children, friends, family, and the community at large. The world has witnessed untold grief caused by out-of-control sexual drives. Paul would certainly caution against sexual sins, but his concerns are not as narrow as some of his heirs have represented them. The power of the sexual drive simply represents all those human appetites that demand satisfaction, refusing to take no for an answer.

Paul's passion is to help and encourage those who are committed to living "by the Spirit." Our model is Jesus himself, "who, though he was in the form of God, did not regard equality with God as something to be exploited, but emptied himself, taking the form of a slave, . . . and became obedient to the point of death—even death on a cross" (*Phil. 2:6–8*). Following this model, believers do not approach life as something they must hurriedly gobble up as in a feeding frenzy.

Rather, life is an opportunity to open one's hands, releasing the gifts God has made available for us to offer one another. To serve our neighbor may mean getting less for ourselves. To contribute to a neighborly society, one may let go of what one might otherwise seize.

To crucify the flesh is not to beat ourselves without mercy. It is, rather, to put to death that shadowy part of our personality that demands satisfaction without regard to the need of our neighbor. Paul, in fact, was echoing the words of the Lord Jesus himself. Jesus had said, "If any want to become my followers, let them deny themselves and take up their cross and follow me" (*Matt. 16:24*). This is not a call to a cheerless life in which we must smother all natural appetites. It is a call to subdue that persistent inner voice that seduces us, lies to us, misrepresents reality, and teaches us the self-justifying speeches that permit us to set ourselves against God, our neighbor, and our own best selves. (Consider *Gen. 3:1*: "Now the serpent was more crafty than any other wild animal that the Lord God had made.")

Guided by the Spirit

So then, brothers and sisters, we are debtors, not to the flesh, to live according to the flesh—for if you will live according to the flesh, you will die; but if by the spirit you put to death the deeds of the body, you will live. For all who are led by the Spirit of God are children of God.
—Romans 8:12–14

When we read the Scriptures today, we usually read them as though they were addressed to individuals. This is a misunderstanding of Scripture. Almost all the Scriptures were addressed to communities—groups of people—rather than to individuals. The advice given is almost always advice to a community. The individual certainly has personal responsibilities, but the individual who strives to "live by the Spirit" is always an individual in community.

There is no question that the Spirit works in individual lives. However, the Spirit was first poured out upon the church (*Acts 2*). In our baptism, God simultaneously receives us into the community of Jesus Christ and pours the Holy Spirit upon us.

Defend, O Lord, your servant N.
with your heavenly grace,
that he/she may continue yours forever,
and daily increase in your Holy Spirit more and more,
until he/she comes to your everlasting kingdom.[4]

We appeal to the Spirit for guidance directly, asking God's help in "crucifying the flesh" and freeing us to live in ways both godly and neighborly. But we also look for the Spirit's help and support as we share in the life of the community of faith: the church. God has gifted the body of Christ with resources through which the Spirit comes to our aid as we struggle to "live by the Spirit." The church continually calls us to discover our own

4. From *Book of Common Worship* (Louisville: Westminster/John Knox Press, 1993), 413.

ministries and offers opportunities for us to exercise them—in the larger community as well as in the church. As we grow into the ministries to which we have been called, we learn step-by-step, as a child learns, "love, joy, peace, patience, kindness, generosity, faithfulness, gentleness, and self-control."

These qualities are not just feelings. They are a positive force that, as we learn them, we project into all our relationships. They are not a burden, but in the practice of these qualities we discover that they bring delight to ourselves as well as to others. "If we live by the Spirit, let us also be guided by the Spirit" (*Gal. 5:25*).

Devote yourself to prayer, keeping alert in it with thanksgiving.
—Colossians 4:2

In the church, a treasury of resources helps us seek the guidance of the Spirit. In every service of worship, we offer to God prayers of thanksgiving and intercession. To offer prayers of gratitude is important—not because God will be offended if we don't send a thank-you note, but because we have a built-in need to express our thanks. In our thanksgivings, we may also direct our attention to all the good things God has given us, rather than focusing too exclusively on the things we lack or on what has gone wrong.

Prayers of intercession are prayers for other people. In both individual and congregational prayer, we turn our hearts toward others. In one of the services in our congregation, those present write down the first names of people or groups of people in need or in crisis. This has become a rich time for us. Praying for another—and having others pray for us—unites us in solidarity with one another and with the Spirit who prays through us.

Another of the community's resources is the Lord's Supper. In the Great Thanksgiving at the Lord's Table, the presiding minister prays that the Holy Spirit may descend upon us and upon the bread and cup. In the Lord's Supper, we believe that the Spirit gathers us with all the believers of every time and place. The Spirit delivers Jesus Christ to us as our spiritual nourishment. This spiritual food strengthens us to live by the Spirit, subduing those shadowy inner impulses that misdirect us and empowering us to embody in our lives and relationships the fruit of the Spirit.

The apostle closes this brief section of his letter with a warning against the temptations of self-righteousness. To the extent that we are successful in crucifying the flesh and exhibiting some of the fruit of the Spirit in our lives, that deceitful inner voice may invite us to feel smug and superior. Paul has foreseen such a possibility and warns, "Let us not become conceited, competing against one another, envying one another" (*Gal. 5:26*). In other words, the

Christian life isn't a competition each against the other. We are in this struggle together. Supporting one another, we may dare to hope that eventually the fruit of the Spirit may become evident in our lives and in the life of our shared community.

Disciplines of the Spirit

Galatians 6:1–10

My friends, if anyone is detected in a transgression, you who have received the Spirit should restore such a one in a spirit of gentleness. Take care that you yourselves are not tempted. Bear one another's burdens, and in this way you will fulfill the law of Christ. For if those who are nothing think they are something, they deceive themselves. All must test their own work; then that work, rather than their neighbor's work, will become a cause for pride. For all must carry their own loads.

Those who are taught the word must share in all good things with their teacher.

Do not be deceived; God is not mocked, for you reap whatever you sow. If you sow to your own flesh, you will reap corruption from the flesh; but if you sow to the Spirit, you will reap eternal life from the Spirit. So let us not grow weary in doing what is right, for we will reap at harvest time, if we do not give up. So then, whenever we have an opportunity, let us work for the good of all, and especially for those of the family of faith.

Confession or Therapy?

Bear one another's burdens, and in this way you will fulfill the law of Christ.
—Galatians 6:2

As a pastor, I have heard a few confessions over the years. What astonishes me is not that there are people who have transgressions they need to confess, but that there are so few! Given the numbers of people for whom I have had pastoral responsibility, it is remarkable how seldom people have come to bare their souls. It may be that the members of the congregations I have served are extraordinarily pure of heart, mind, body, and spirit. Or it may be that they have found others with whom to share their burdens. Or it may be that many of us are too proud to let anyone who knows us see those parts of our lives that we prefer to keep hidden.

We live in a time when people troubled by a guilty conscience are more likely to resort to a psychotherapist than to a minister, elder, or fellow church member. We pay the therapist to listen to our story. Perhaps it's the purely professional relationship that makes it easier to tell all. It is, in a way, an impersonal transaction, similar to going to one's personal physician or dentist. The therapist has no particular moral expectations of us, so presumably will be neither shocked nor disappointed. We can tell our therapist what we would never want our minister (or fellow church member) to know.

I am grateful for mental health professionals—therapists and counselors of all sorts and descriptions. Frequently I refer people to their care because they have expertise that I don't have in treating those who are ill. However, not everyone who feels burdened with a guilty conscience has a neurosis or a personality disorder that requires the care of a professional therapist.

In fact, a good deal of the anguish with which many of us live is the result of some evil we have, in fact, done—or some good thing left undone. In other words, we have a spiritual problem rather than simply an emotional one. The therapeutic remedy may fit an emotional problem, while leaving the spiritual problem untreated.

The Need for a Listening Ear

Therefore confess your sins to one another, and pray for one another, so that you may be healed. The prayer of the righteous is powerful and effective.
—*James 5:16*

If we confess our sins, he who is faithful and just will forgive us our sins and cleanse us from all unrighteousness.
—*1 John 1:9*

The medieval Roman Catholic Church required its members to go to a priest to make a confession and receive absolution before going to communion. One's confession was anonymous; the face of the person confessing was hidden from the person hearing the confession. In the formative years of Protestantism, the Reformers abolished the confessional. However, it was not because they believed there was no value in making a personal confession. The Reformers' intention was to substitute face-to-face meetings at the initiative of church members or at the initiative of pastors who sensed a need. (The Prayer of Confession used in most of our public services served an entirely different purpose, and the Reformers didn't intend that it be a substitute for the confessional.) We use the term pastoral care to describe what the Reformers had in mind.

In his book *Life Together*, Dietrich Bonhoeffer writes about how important it is that a Christian be able to confess as specifically and concretely as possible to a brother or sister in the faith. He is doubtful that in any community there can be only one such person who hears such confessions. In fact, he argues, any Christian who knows what it is to have tried and failed can serve as one who hears the confession of another. Any sinner can listen to whatever hard thing must be confessed and can voice a word of forgiveness with confidence on behalf of Jesus Christ. Ordination is not required![5]

But why isn't it just as good to confess one's sins directly to God? Bonhoeffer reasons that when we imagine that we are confessing directly to God, and receiving God's pardon directly,

5. Dietrich Bonhoeffer, *Life Together* (New York and Evanston: Harper & Row, Publishers, Inc., 1954).

iBelieve

very often the result is a futile gesture to pardon ourselves. That's why the same temptation rises over and over again to plague us. When we take the risk of confessing openly and boldly to a fellow Christian, and receiving from our brother or sister assurance of God's pardon, we are far more likely to break free of the behaviors causing us grief.

Confession and pardon are a far different remedy from psychotherapy. In confession and pardon, the remedy is the assurance that God, in Christ, has washed away the burden of our guilt. The remedy is not to deny guilt, to justify behavior, or to encourage rationalizations. The remedy is the confident promise that Christ, the healer, is at work to heal us.

We often hear that confession is good for the soul. Why is that so?

What is the difference between confessing to God and confessing to a human being?

How is confession between Christians different from talking with a professional therapist?

What is the function of the Prayer of Confession in the service of worship?

My friends, if anyone is detected in a transgression, you who have received the Spirit should restore such a one in a spirit of gentleness. Take care that you yourselves are not tempted. Bear one another's burdens, and in this way you will fulfill the law of Christ.

—Galatians 6:1–2

Here is a biblical mandate for taking responsibility for one another. The mandate is not addressed to ministers only, or to elders or deacons only, but to all Christian people. And yet, if we were to take the mandate seriously, wouldn't it be as though we had a license to act as busybodies, interfering with each other's privacy?

When challenged to take responsibility for another, people used to quote Scripture, asking, rhetorically, "Am I my brother's keeper?" They presumed that clearly they were not. However, the quotation actually occurs after Cain has murdered his brother Abel. God asks Cain where his brother is. Cain replies that he does not know, and then, rather insolently, asks God: "Am I my brother's keeper?" (*Gen. 4:9*). The answer to the question, from God's point of view, is clearly "Yes!" Cain does have a responsibility for his brother.

If asked to justify our philosophy of "live and let live," many would do so on the basis of tolerance. We live, after all, in a society that values broad-mindedness. However, what passes for tolerance might just as easily be indifference. And why wouldn't we be indifferent to the behavior of our neighbors—even our brothers and sisters in Christ? In recent decades, we have been shocked so often as to have become shockproof. Watergate, the sexual revolution, the boldness of the entertainment media, closer acquaintance with people of other cultures, seasons of unparalleled prosperity, anonymous urban or suburban living—all have contributed to the numbing of our sensitivities. We may not be sure ourselves where tolerance leaves off and indifference begins. Whatever we may think about the way our neighbor lives, we simply close our mouths and avert our eyes.

Intervention

My friends, if anyone is detected in a transgression, you who have received the Spirit should restore such a one in a spirit of gentleness. Take care that you yourselves are not tempted. Bear one another's burdens, and in this way you will fulfill the law of Christ.
—*Galatians 6:1–2*

One can imagine, I suppose, at the distance of nearly twenty centuries, how Christian brothers and sisters in one of the cities of Galatia might have drawn one another aside for a heart-to-heart talk about their behavior. It is even possible to imagine how an older member of one's own church might take aside a teenager or very young adult for an honest confrontation. However, it is almost impossible to imagine one adult church member speaking directly to another about his or her conduct. Such an intervention would seem a terrible invasion of privacy—a risk of offending that few would dare to take.

It's almost—but not entirely—impossible to imagine such a thing. For example, "interventions" have begun to become accepted ways of dealing with people addicted to alcohol or drugs. When it became obvious that a member of a certain congregation had become dependent on alcohol, her friends and family organized an intervention. Her two daughters, her son, her pastor, and her physician agreed on a time to meet in her home. They confronted the woman—a faithful church member—with evidence of her dependency. They described its effects on them and on other members of the family. They assured her of their love and their devotion. They promised to stand by her. They spoke to her clearly about the remedies available. When she agreed to a course of treatment, they took her immediately and by prearrangement to the treatment facility that was prepared to admit her.

An intervention of this sort is a risky business. It is not impossible that even close observers might be wrong in their assessment of the situation. The person for whom they have organized the intervention may, despite assurances, see those who have intervened as hostile and mean-spirited and refuse all

iBelieve

pleas to accept the help offered. The intervention may end in a standoff that results in bitterness and alienation. Still, those who love the person take all those risks. They take risks out of love and concern for their mother or father, friend, son, daughter, parishioner, or patient.

The love and respect one feels for a friend or family member in the grip of an addiction is an active love—not a sentimental affection. Friends and family members see the one they love in an exposed position. Individuals who are addicted to alcohol or drugs destroy or distort relationships, disfigure their own personalities, and put themselves and others in danger. One might put up an argument that one should "live and let live." The alternative is for those near to the person to take responsibility for their neighbor.

In a Spirit of Gentleness

Have nothing to do with stupid and senseless controversies; you know that they breed quarrels. And the Lord's servant must not be quarrelsome but kindly to everyone, an apt teacher, patient, correcting opponents with gentleness. God may perhaps grant that they will repent and come to know the truth, and that they may escape from the snare of the devil, having been held captive by him to do his will.

—2 Timothy 2:23–26

Dependence on alcohol and drugs is sure to be destructive. Is it possible that certain kinds of behaviors, though not destructive to the body, are destructive to the soul? Paul produced a whole list of such behaviors in his letter to the Galatians (*Gal. 5:19–21*). He believed that what he called "the works of the flesh" would inevitably lead to spiritual destruction (*Gal. 5:21*). Do you suppose it would be possible to make a case for intervention when one Christian sees another Christian engaging in behavior that is caustic to the spirit?

Consider these situations:

- You have served on the worship committee of your local congregation with a man who showed great devotion to the faith and to the church. When you were traveling on business in another city, you encountered this man in a hotel with a woman who was not his wife. Flustered, he took you aside and begged you not to mention this back home. What do you do?

- A few years ago, you served as a youth adviser with a woman who is now a member of the city zoning council. Through contacts in the construction business, you learn that she has been taking gifts of money in return for a favorable vote on certain development projects. What do you do?

- Someone who sings in the same church choir as you has developed a reputation for fomenting controversy. He has embittered the choir director against the worship committee and the pastor. He has divided his adult Bible study group—half of them refuse to come any longer. Picking up on issues being

iBelieve

debated in the denomination, he has vilified church officers. What do you do?

One thing is for sure: You can't simply report these people to the pastor and turn your back. The obligation to look out for one another's spiritual health is not one that can be delegated to someone paid to do such things. Paul wrote to all the Christians of the Galatian churches: "My friends, if anyone is detected in a transgression, you who have received the Spirit should restore such a one in a spirit of gentleness" (*Gal. 6:1*). I have known church members with the courage and the sensitivity required to handle such problems head-on. When I am the one who has witnessed the behaviors in question, then I am the one best equipped to deal with the situation. How do I do that? Paul spells out his method with crystal clarity: "in a spirit of gentleness."

Neither Judgmental nor Indifferent

Why do you pass judgment on your brother or sister? Or you, why do you despise your brother or sister? For we will all stand before the judgment seat of God. For it is written, "As I live, says the Lord, every knee shall bow to me, and every tongue shall give praise to God." So then, each of us will be accountable to God.

—Romans 14:10–12

Most of us are terrified of being—or appearing to be— "judgmental." We know only too well Jesus' warning, "Do not judge, so that you may not be judged" (*Matt. 7:1*). In fact, only those who are keenly aware of their own vulnerability should dare to warn another Christian—and then only cautiously, in fear and trembling, and with prayer. Our work is not to judge, but, as Paul put it, to "restore." Our interest is not in finding fault, but in helping the other to recognize the peril into which he or she has fallen. If judging is wrong, then indifference to that peril is equally wrong. The only motivation for confronting another Christian is concern for the life and well-being of the neighbor—and for the well-being of the community of faith we share.

Paul wrote, "Bear one another's burdens, and in this way you will fulfill the law of Christ" (*Gal. 6:2*). The "law of Christ" is not a written code. The law of Christ is to love, and the strength that empowers that love is the Spirit. Those who, in love, take their neighbor's well-being seriously will also welcome those who give them objective feedback about themselves.

"Take care that you yourselves are not tempted" (*Gal. 6:1b*). The first obligation of any serious Christian is to test oneself. Seeing the spiritual peril that threatens my neighbor is far easier. One way of defining what it is to be a "sinner" is that I lack objectivity about myself. In other words, I am likely to see my actions in a favorable light even when an impartial observer does not. The serious Christian will welcome a brother or sister who offers the gift of an objective appraisal—as long as it is without judgment.

No sin is so deep-seated and pervasive as self-deception. Paul encourages us to scrutinize ourselves at precisely this point. "For if those who are nothing think they are something, they deceive themselves. All must test their own work" (*Gal. 6:3–4a*).

Consider the meaning of Galatians 6:2 in a day when violence seems closer to home than ever and many families reside a far distance from other family members.

How are we to bear one another's burdens?

How do you see this verse connected to the fruit of the Spirit? to the works of the flesh?

Further Thoughts

Day 36 Discipleship

In his letter to the churches of Galatia, the apostle Paul does not use the word *discipline,* or even the word *disciple,* to which it is related. His letter is an almost angry response to developments in the Galatian churches. Some unknown preachers, whom Bible scholars have called "Judaizers," were preaching a very different gospel than the one Paul preached to them. The Judaizers tried to teach the Galatians that they had an obligation to keep certain parts of the Jewish Torah, or Law. Paul argues forcefully that anyone who attempts to please God by keeping rules completely misunderstands the gospel. The coming of Jesus Christ has made the Old Testament law obsolete. God has called us to be members of the household of God, and has done so without imposing any conditions.

What are the implications of this? If Christians have been set free from commandments and rules, has God liberated them from the obligation to live moral lives? Paul says not. However, it is not a written code that governs Christians, but the requirement of love. Far from reducing their responsibilities, the call to love expands them. But how can mortal beings, so troubled by human temptations, live lives characterized by love? Paul argues that the Holy Spirit makes such a thing possible. The Spirit provides a power beyond our imagining to help us to do what God in Christ has called us to do. The God who called us to be disciples will, by the Spirit, enable us to grow.

Those who want to impress others by means of the flesh are trying to compel you to be circumcised. The only reason they do this is to avoid being persecuted for the cross of Christ. Not even those who are circumcised keep the law, yet they want you to be circumcised that they may boast about your circumcision in the flesh. May I never boast except in the cross of our Lord Jesus Christ, through which the world has been crucified to me, and I to the world. Neither circumcision nor uncircumcision means anything; what counts is the new creation. Peace and mercy to all who follow this rule—to the Israel of God. From now on, let no one cause me trouble, for I bear on my body the marks of Jesus. The grace of our Lord Jesus Christ be with your spirit, brothers and sisters. Amen.
—Galatians 6:12–18 (TNIV)

No human being can say precisely how God's Spirit works in us—as a community, or as individuals. Yet the church's experience has been that the Spirit works through discipline and through disciplines. It does not work exclusively through these means, but reliably. The Spirit works for our strength and benefit through discipline—the mutual care of church members for one another, and the oversight of those chosen to be leaders in the church. The Spirit also works for our strength and benefit through disciplines—those practices and resources that we seek to incorporate into our routines until they virtually become "habits of the heart."

It is difficult to live in a community of faith that we are willing to take so seriously that we yield to it some of our personal autonomy. We know that communities can misuse authority. They can be abusive, and they can misdirect us. Those who make a sober assessment of themselves know as well that we are not sufficient unto ourselves. We desperately need community—not just companionship, but the kind of support that comes only when we share our lives more than superficially.

If Christians have been set free from commandments and rules, are we thus liberated from the obligation to lead moral lives?

Of course not.

"Lord, Make Us Servants of Your Peace"

Bless those who persecute you; bless and do not curse them. Rejoice with those who rejoice, weep with those who weep. Live in harmony with one another; do not be haughty, but associate with the lowly; do not claim to be wiser than you are. Do not repay anyone evil for evil, but take thought for what is noble in the sight of all. If it is possible, so far as it depends on you, live peaceably with all.

—Romans 12:14–18

1. Lord, make us servants of Your peace:
   Where there is hate, may we sow love;
   Where there is hurt, may we forgive;
   Where there is strife, may we make one.

2. Where all is doubt, may we sow faith;
   Where all is gloom, may we sow hope;
   Where all is night, may we sow light;
   Where all is tears, may we sow joy.

3. Jesus, our Lord, may we not seek
   To be consoled, but to console,
   Nor look to understanding hearts,
   But look for hearts to understand.

4. May we not look for love's return,
   But seek to love unselfishly,
   For in our giving we receive,
   And in forgiving are forgiven.

5. Dying, we live, and are reborn
   Through death's dark night to endless day:
   Lord, make us servants of Your peace
   To wake at last in heaven's light.[6]

6. Text: © James Quinn, S.J. Reprinted by permission of Geoffrey Chapman, a division of Cassell Publishers, London.

iBelieve

Don't Get Tired of Doing the Right Thing

. . . but those who hope in the LORD will renew their strength. They will soar on wings like eagles; they will run and not grow weary, they will walk and not be faint.

—*Isaiah 40:31 (TNIV)*

"So let us not grow weary in doing what is right," Paul wrote, "for we will reap at harvest time, if we do not give up" (*Gal. 6:9*). Paul brought his letter to the Galatians to a climax with these words that point to the coming day of judgment. His words are not meant to frighten, but to encourage the Galatians to look with confidence to that great day. It will be a day of confirmation, when those who have sought to live in the Spirit "will reap eternal life from the Spirit" (*Gal. 6:8*). "So then," Paul concludes, "whenever we have an opportunity, let us work for the good of all, and especially for those of the family of faith" (*Gal. 6:10*).

This is a summons to serve the community of Jesus Christ, though that service may prove scary and risky. We are, after all, supported by God's grace—not by the prospect of successfully avoiding all mistakes or every spiritual pitfall. The Christian life is not meant to be a timid affair, but a bold and courageous one. If, in our boldness, we commit an offense, God's promise is that "we may receive mercy and find grace to help in time of need" (*Heb. 4:16*).

One of the most important spiritual disciplines we undertake will be the discipline of service—beginning with, but not limited to, "the family of faith." In "bearing one another's burdens," we look for ways to support one another and to find support. That support may take the form of mutual admonition. It may take the form of finding within the church a person or people in whom we can confide and from whom we can receive the assurance of God's pardon.

It will certainly include having a concern for those who are most vulnerable, and in turn welcoming the concern of those who see our vulnerabilities more clearly than we can.

Concern for the vulnerable includes concern for the children and youth among us. It is certain that our concern for "the family of faith"—and for its weaker members—will also lead some of us to activism in the larger community.

Our spiritual discipline may take the form of service on a school board or a planning commission. A discipline of the spirit may include writing letters to the editor of a newspaper or lobbying in the state legislature.

Every spiritual discipline requires energy and determination. In time, our energy may diminish. Nevertheless, even when it seems as though our efforts have not been as successful as we would like, the Spirit will restore our souls. "So let us not grow weary in doing what is right, for we will reap at harvest time, if we do not give up" (*Gal. 6:9*).

"Give to the Winds Thy Fears"

. . . . do not fear, for I am with you, do not be afraid, for I am your God; I will strengthen you, I will help you, I will uphold you with my victorious right hand.

—Isaiah 41:10

1. Give to the winds thy fears;
   Hope and be undismayed:
   God hears thy sighs and counts thy tears,
   God shall lift up thy head.

2. Through waves and clouds and storms
   God gently clears thy way;
   Wait patiently; so shall this night
   Soon end in joyous day.

3. Leave to God's sovereign sway
   To choose and to command;
   So shalt thou, wondering, own God's way,
   How wise, how strong God's hand!

4. On God the Lord rely,
   And safe shalt thou go on;
   Fix on God's work thy steadfast eye,
   So shall thy work be done.[7]

Prayer:

O God,
light of the minds that know you,
life of the souls that love you,
strength of the thoughts that seek you:
Help us so to know you
that we may truly love you,
so to love you
that we may fully serve you,

---

7. "Give to the Winds Thy Fears," *The Presbyterian Hymnal* (Louisville: Westminster/ John Knox Press, 1990), no. 286.

iBelieve

whose service is perfect freedom;
through Jesus Christ our Lord,
who lives and reigns with you and the Holy Spirit,
one God, now and forever. Amen.[8]

---

8. *Book of Common Worship* (Louisville: Westminster/John Knox Press, 1993), p. 360.

iBelieve

I Believe:
40 Daily Readings
for the Purposeful Presbyterian

The Shape of the Christian Life

SMALL-GROUP STUDY GUIDE
By Carol Wehrheim

Introduction

This guide is designed to aid group study by providing five session plans for use during your reading of *I Believe: 40 Daily Readings for the Purposeful Presbyterian*. These session plans include a variety of educational methods; the leader of the group study will have the responsibility of choosing the methods that are most appropriate to your group. Each participant in the study should have a copy of this book and should make a commitment to participating in each session. As you prepare to lead the group study, you will want to:

- Read the daily entries.

- Skim through this study guide, noting any activity that will require advance preparation.

- Obtain teaching and learning resources recommended in the session plans, such as newsprint and markers, masking tape, *The Presbyterian Hymnal,* the *Book of Common Worship,* paper, and pencils.

- Focus on the main idea.

- Prepare the meeting space, based on your leadership style. For example, a circle of chairs is conducive to a leader who seeks to foster an open discussion; chairs around a table offer a good space for writing and discussion; and a lectern facing a block of chairs works best for a lecture presentation.

- Pray for the Holy Spirit's guidance.

Coordinating Daily Devotionals and Study Sessions

It will be important for the participants to be on the same page, as it were. Consider calling the group together for an orientation to the study at least one week before the first session. During this orientation session, distribute copies of the book to the participants. Prepare a reading schedule for distribution to the group; for example, if your group meets on Sundays:

Sunday, (*insert date here*): Read Day 1

Monday, (*insert date here*): Read Day 2

Tuesday, (*insert date here*): Read Day 3

Wednesday, (*insert date here*): Read Day 4

Thursday, (*insert date here*): Read Day 5

Friday, (*insert date here*): Read Day 6

Saturday, (*insert date here*): Read Day 7

Sunday, (*insert date here*): Study Session 1; Read Day 8 . . . etc.

Also note for the group that five additional daily readings (Days 36–40) follow Session 5. You may agree as a group to meet a final time after Day 40 to evaluate the book and the study sessions. This could also be a time of worship and celebration for your group.

For future study options, please visit www.pcusa.org/witherspoon for additional titles in the *I Believe* series.

SMALL-GROUP STUDY
For discussion of Days 1–7 in the daily reader;
to be used after Day 7

Theological Disciplines

FOCUS

The crucial importance—and necessity—of the community of
faith (the church) in the formation of our faith.

MAIN IDEAS

Engagement with the church should be a primary influence in
the formation of one's personal theology. This is in sharp contrast
to the post-Enlightenment culture of today. Our society invests
almost all value in the individual and nearly always suspects
the community. In arguing for the priority of the community,
the prevailing doctrine of personal autonomy is challenged. The
church—the community of faith that transcends space and time—
has the authority to teach us what the gospel really is. Paul
claimed the authority of revelation. The church has received
his letter to the Galatians because it recognized in this writing
the gospel it has heard and believed from the beginning. In the
Scripture, we discover the church's faith and trust it.

PREPARING TO LEAD

* Explore how truth is determined.
    * ❏ Where do you turn to discover truth? Do you rely on
      yourself, perhaps on a gut feeling, or do you seek the
      counsel of others? A variety of possibilities are named
      in "I Believe What the Church Believes" (Day 3).
    * ❏ On what might the Galatians be basing their decision
      about truth? On what does Paul base his?
    * ❏ Read John 18:33–38. What is the truth that Jesus is
      speaking to Pilate?
* Explore the argument Paul has with the Judaizers, who have
  persuaded some of the Galatians that they must follow Jewish
  law in order to be Christians.

- ❏ Paul is a Jew, yet he says that the Galatians, who are Gentiles, are foolish because "having started with the Spirit," they are "now ending with the flesh" (*Gal. 3:3*). What is his reasoning here?

- ❏ Also see Galatians 3:19–29. Note that this is an "interchurch" argument. The Judaizers are Jews who believe that Christ is the Messiah. However, they also believe that to follow Christ, one must take on all the Jewish laws. The Jerusalem Council has already decided that this is not necessary (*Acts 15*), basing their decision on Peter's visions on the rooftop and the conversion of Cornelius (*Acts 10*).

- • Explore the ecclesiology (doctrine of the church) that Paul is espousing in the letter to the Galatians.

  - ❏ Who is the church for Paul? What is the role of the church for him?

  - ❏ How does Paul's view compare with your own, particularly in the matter of the role or influence of the church on individual members?

  - ❏ What impact might such a view have in a society that is highly individualistic?

GATHERING ACTIVITIES

(Use as appropriate.)

- • Provide each person with a sheet of blank paper and a pencil. Have the participants draw at least three concentric circles on the paper. In the center circle, instruct the participants to write their names. In the next circle, have them write the names of people they know who influence or help form their faith. In the third circle, have them write people or groups they do not know personally but who influence their faith formation. Have them continue to move from the personal to think of people or groups who exert influence on them. When everyone is finished, call for categories of persons or groups for each circle and print these on concentric circles on newsprint. For example, the second circle might be parents, grandparents, pastors, and church schoolteachers, and the third circle might be curriculum writers.

- The writer points out the value of a faith mentor. As a group, prepare a job description for a faith mentor based on the material in the daily reader and the ideas of group members. Print the description on newsprint. Perhaps some group members have been mentors or sponsors for young people in confirmation class. Ask about that experience and have the group compare it to the prepared job description.

- Spiritual disciplines are important to our faith development. Together, create a list of spiritual disciplines and print it on newsprint. Note that each session during this study includes a different spiritual practice.

GUIDING THE DISCUSSION

- Have the group members silently recall the people or groups who have been instrumental in their faith formation.

- Ask the group: As you have grown in faith, how have you determined what voices to pay attention to and which to ignore? Invite them to talk about the voices that were not helpful and those that were.

- Read Galatians 1:1–12 silently or aloud. Ask the following:
    - ❐ What is the authority that Paul claims?
    - ❐ On what does he base this authority?
    - ❐ How can Paul be so certain that he has the truth?
    - ❐ Scan Galatians 1:13—2:14. Paul takes the time to detail his experiences and the decisions of the Jerusalem

Council. Why is this important to his case before the Galatians? Notice how early in the life of the church disagreements began!

- Few Christians today claim a revelation from God or Jesus Christ. Ask the following:
  - ❐ How does the church help you determine what truth is?
  - ❐ What do you do when there are contradictions in the Bible or church doctrine?
  - ❐ Where else do you discover truth or find help to discern what is true?

- Conclude this discussion by summarizing the definition of truth that has surfaced in the discussion. Suggest that the group reflect on that definition until the next session to see if it continues to work for them.

OPTIONAL ACTIVITIES

- Debate: Divide the participants into two groups. Label one the supporters of Paul, and label the other the Judaizers. Have each group prepare arguments for its position. Suggest that the participants look through the rest of Galatians as they prepare. Hold the debate so both sides can be heard by the entire group.

- Spiritual discipline: The "discipline" of reading Scripture in the company of fellow believers of all generations is critical to sustaining the Christian life. Read Galatians 1:1–2 aloud. In these two verses, Paul sets the stage for the authority he has for writing this letter. How does he do that? What does his self-description stress?

NOTES:

SMALL-GROUP STUDY
For discussion of Days 8–14 in the daily reader;
to be used after Day 14

Disciplines of Love

FOCUS

The requirement of the disciplines of love on us to accept God's love, freely given, and to respond to love by giving freely to others.

MAIN IDEAS

The "normal" sense of what is fair is that in every transaction there should be an equal exchange. In other words, we pay for whatever we get, and vice versa. Christian faith—as clarified in Paul's argument with the Judaizers—is that God has invited us to be part of God's household with no strings attached. In traditional theological language, we are saved entirely by the free grace of God, not by any merit of our own. God saves us out of sheer generosity, rooted in love. However, God's grace, poured liberally on us, rightfully evokes a response of gratitude. We learn to love God and one another. This love is not a feeling, but something we do. God has freed us from obsessive rule-keeping and scorekeeping in order that we may be a blessing to our neighbors.

Disciplines that encourage love are disciplines of stewardship, the gifts of our time and talents. A related, and often neglected, discipline is being able to receive graciously. Receiving others' love and care is one more way of taming the pride that claims that we can do it all ourselves. Receiving graciously from those around us prepares us to receive the gift of God's grace and love.

PREPARING TO LEAD

- Explore how the Christian faith calls us to act in ways that seem counter to the cultural norms.
    - ❐ Discuss the essay by Judge Tomei (Day 9). What were the dynamics in the story? How did God intervene? What groundwork was necessary for God's intervention to take hold?

❑ How do we prepare ourselves to be such a conduit of God's love and mercy?

- Explore the definition of God's justice as put forth in the article.

  ❑ How is it different from the fair-trade justice that we generally seek? How does Paul define God's justice in the argument with the Judaizers operating in the churches in Galatia? How is God's grace a part of God's justice?

  ❑ See the definition of grace in "Christian Faith Is Peculiar" (Day 10). How would operating from this understanding of justice change your life?

- Explore the mind of Jesus Christ as a model for conducting oneself as a Christian.

  ❑ Read Galatians 5:6, a key verse to understanding the mind of Jesus Christ. Also turn to "Peculiar, but Not Stupid!" (Day 11), looking especially at the third paragraph. What are the new ways of seeing and reasoning that the church coaches us in?

  ❑ Read Matthew 20:1–16 (the parable of the laborers in the vineyard). How does this parable interpret God's justice or the mind of Jesus Christ?

GATHERING ACTIVITIES
(Use as appropriate.)

- Distribute paper and pens or pencils to each participant. Invite each person to create abstract diagrams that demonstrate the connection between grace, love, and faith. Examples might include a triangle with words *grace, love,* and *faith* at each point or a stair-step diagram with the words *grace, love,* and *faith* associated with a particular step. Ask the participants to try to represent the interconnectedness between

iBelieve

the three words/concepts in their diagrams. When all have completed the task, invite them to compare their efforts.

- Write the words *grace, love, freedom,* and *faith* on newsprint. During the session, print the definitions as the group develops them. Having succinct definitions before them will help the participants use these words with more precision.

GUIDING THE DISCUSSION

- Recruit group members to read Galatians 5:2–15 aloud from at least two different translations. During the readings, have the participants listen without following in their Bibles. Pause for a moment of silence before the second reading.

- Ask the group for initial reactions to this passage. What stood out for them? What surprised them?

  ❏ Look more carefully at verse 13. Refer to "Love Is Something You Do" (Day 13). What is the connection between freedom and love?

  ❏ The writer notes that the Greek word translated as "become slaves" has the sense of providing loving service. How would you interpret this verse for others? What guidance does it give you as you try to "be in the Lord"?

- Move to verse 14 and have the participants discuss love as a response to God's gift of grace.

  ❏ Ask: What is the basis of our response in love? Note the insistence in the article on a definition of love as an act rather than a feeling.

  ❏ Continue by recalling the story about building the house in "There's Community in Giving" (Day 14).

❏ Ask the following: When have you taken part in this kind of giving love? When have you been the recipient of, and graciously accepted, such giving love?

• Finally, discuss the meaning of faith in this passage.

❏ Read aloud verse 6. Have the group refer to "There's Community in Giving" (Day 14).

❏ In a sentence, how does the author define *faith*? What is the connection between faith and love and grace?

OPTIONAL ACTIVITIES

• Sculptures: Provide small boxes of many sizes, foam packing pieces, craft sticks, and any other materials you have for the group members to create sculptures showing love, grace, or faith. Hot-glue guns or white glue will make the work faster for this project. If possible, have the participants spray their sculptures with dark gray or black paint, covering the entire sculpture.

• Spiritual discipline: Hospitality as a spiritual discipline is one way of providing loving service for others. Hospitality is both receiving from the other person and giving to the other person. Have the participants think of a specific time when they received the hospitality of another person or when they gave to another person. Then invite them to ponder how that occasion showed God's hospitality as the giver of grace and love. For more on hospitality as a spiritual discipline, see "Entertaining Angels Unawares: The Spirit of Hospitality," in *Soul Feast* by Marjorie J. Thompson (Louisville: Westminster/ John Knox Press, 1995).

• Line out a psalm: Psalm 117 is short, but it expresses the joy that accompanies our response to God's gift of grace. Say each line for the group to repeat. Say the lines with joy and fervor, and ask the group to repeat them in the same manner.

SMALL-GROUP STUDY
For discussion of Days 15–21 in the daily reader;
to be used after Day 21

$\mathcal{S}$ession 3

Disciplining the Flesh

FOCUS
The meaning of Paul's admonition to "live by the Spirit"
(*Gal. 5:16a*).

MAIN IDEAS
In Paul's terminology, "the flesh" may refer primarily to temptations rooted in our physical selves, but generally his use of this term has a broader meaning. Our whole selves—not just our bodies—are subject to temptation. Our so-called higher faculties (intellect and spiritual selves) can also mislead us. Even when we know the right thing, we often find ourselves doing exactly the opposite. We are good at self-justification, but we really cannot explain why our better selves so often lose this conflict that takes place within us. Paul contrasts flesh with Spirit, exhorting his readers to "live by the Spirit." One way the Spirit works is through the church, either through bodies established to guide its officers and members or through informal relationships that serve a similar purpose. The Spirit enables us to respond to God's grace with gratitude and with graciousness toward others. The Spirit represents God's personal, sustaining relationship with us. Differing from an impersonal code of law, the Spirit represents God's intimate care for us and God's will that we succeed in living the Christian life. Spiritual disciplines help us live out of our best selves—the thankful parts of ourselves— rather than the shadowy parts of ourselves. An important spiritual discipline in this regard is prayer, both individual and communal. Another is the continual remembering of our baptism, through which God claimed us and solemnly promised to be our God forever.

PREPARING TO LEAD
- Explore the longings that are promoted by society.
  - ❏ Refer to those areas named in "The 'Flesh' " (Day 16). What longings do they produce?

i*B*elieve

95

- ❏ If there are a number of parents or grandparents in the group, the discussion might turn to ways that we teach children to evaluate the promotion of longings. This discussion could, of course, also benefit adults.
- ❏ How might the list Paul includes in Galatians 5:19–21 be revised to include the longings named by the group?
- ❏ Do some items in Paul's list seem more offensive than others? Why?
- Explore Galatians 5:16.
  - ❏ What does it mean to "live by the Spirit"? As you explore this question, refer to " 'Flesh' versus Spirit" (Day 17).
  - ❏ Does living by the Spirit remove the need for the law? Why or why not? How would you explain this concept to a new Christian or to a teenager?
- Explore how Paul has experienced what he is writing.
  - ❏ How was his personal experience of Jesus Christ like living "in the Spirit"?
  - ❏ What was his relationship with the law before his conversion on the road to Damascus (see *Gal. 1:13ff*)? If the group is not familiar with this story, read Acts 9:1–19.
  - ❏ What can we draw for ourselves from Paul's experience?

GATHERING ACTIVITIES
(Use as appropriate.)
- On newsprint, list ways to build a personal relationship with God. Review the discussions and the articles from the previous sessions to garner ideas from them. Post the list for the remainder of the study and add to it as new ideas are presented. Be sure the group includes prayers of confession in the list.

- To keep the differences between a personal relationship with God and an impersonal code clearly defined and before the group, list them on newsprint. This might be done as a way to review the article or as the differences surface during the group discussion. A group member might be assigned this task.

GUIDING THE DISCUSSION

- Read Galatians 5:16–21 from at least two translations as described for the Bible reading from the previous sessions.
- Read verse 16 again. Ask: What does it mean to live by the Spirit? During this discussion, refer to the points in "What Can We Rely On?" (Day 19).
  - ☐ Do you think the Spirit can work through the oversight and admonitions of the church, whatever the governing body? Why or why not?
  - ☐ How does the corporate prayer of confession or personal prayers of confession fit into this discussion?
- Define "the flesh" as Paul uses it.
  - ☐ "The flesh" is not exactly the way we would talk about this matter today. What other words or phrases might get at Paul's meaning more clearly?
  - ☐ How is this translated in other Bibles? Which words make the clearest translation for our society?
- What message do you take from Galatians 5:16–21, titled in many Bibles as "The Works of the Flesh"?
- Conclude the discussion with a time for quiet individual reflection.

OPTIONAL ACTIVITIES

- Ads: Provide newspapers and magazines for the group to find ads and promotions that are aimed at "the flesh." Group their findings according to the categories named by Paul or the group.

- Collage: Instead of grouping the ads by category, invite the group to create a collage. On a poster-board backing, glue the ads in a random style so they overlap. Add a title that presents the theme. Display this at the next session as a way to review this discussion.

NOTES:

SMALL-GROUP STUDY
For discussion of Days 22–28 in the daily reader;
to be used after Day 28

Session 4

Spiritual Disciplines

FOCUS

What it means to live by the Spirit, and guided by the Spirit.

MAIN IDEAS

Paul does not argue that the Torah (the Law of God) does not tell the truth about how God wants us to live. He argues, rather, that no system that commits our salvation to our own hands can possibly be successful. The law shows us what we ought to do, but it cannot save us. We are saved by God's grace. Hence, our salvation is in God's hands, not our own.

In Galatians 5:22ff, Paul lists what he calls the "fruit of the Spirit," nine qualities that describe the Christian life as it ought to look. These qualities are the evidence that we live by the Spirit. Yet we strive for them out of loving gratitude, not as evidence of our prowess in mastering a system. They are not emotions, but positive forces to be projected into the world. To live this way, we turn to specific disciplines that open us to the Spirit. Prayer, particularly prayers of thanksgiving and intercession, is part of our repertoire of necessary spiritual disciplines.

Our participation in the Lord's Supper is another. In it, we pray for the Spirit to bless us and the gifts of bread and wine. Here, by the power of the Spirit, God gives us Jesus Christ as spiritual food. However, Paul recognizes that living by the Spirit is not easy. He and Luther, who advised Christians to "sin boldly," are much aware of our failure to exhibit the qualities by which we desire to live. Paul's call is to let go of our frightened, insecure grip on life that prevents us from opening our hand to our neighbor. We are to put that part of ourselves to death. The Christian life is one in which we cheer one another on, resisting the temptation to be smug when we achieve some modicum of success. We are in this together!

iBelieve

PREPARING TO LEAD

- Explore the connection between the list of good qualities in Galatians 5:22–23 and the law that Paul is so upset about in the earlier portions of this letter.

  - ☐ How might the list lead the people back to following the letter of the law? How might it help them avoid that?

  - ☐ Might some interpret this portion of the letter as a new law from Paul? Why or why not? How does Paul counter that possibility?

- Explore Luther's admonishment to "sin boldly."

  - ☐ How might that be interpreted as living in the Spirit? What did Luther mean by this? (See "Sin Boldly" [Day 25] for the writer's interpretation.)

- What might we do when we do not agree on what we should not be doing?

GATHERING ACTIVITIES

(Use as appropriate.)

- Have the participants brainstorm a list of "appetites" as referred to by the writer in "Crucifying the Flesh" (Day 26): "The power of the sexual drive simply represents all those human appetites that demand satisfaction, refusing to take no for an answer." Print their list on newsprint. If the group made the collage suggested in Optional Activities for Session 3, display it as a visual cue for the brainstorming. Remind the participants that they should build on what someone else says in brainstorming, but not evaluate what goes on the paper. When they have finished, look at the list for obvious groups or categories. Which appetites do they find most enticing? Where do they find support for resisting them?

- Draw a horizontal line on a sheet of newsprint. At one end, print *law*; at the other end, print *freedom*. Have the group suggest possibilities for points on the line between the two.

GUIDING THE DISCUSSION
- Read Galatians 5:22–26 from at least two translations as in the previous sessions.
- Focus on verses 22–23.
  - ❏ How do you interpret these fruits of the Spirit today? Would the outcome of them look different today than they did in Paul's day?
  - ❏ Which of these attributes are valued by our society? Are they valued equally for men as for women?
  - ❏ How do you connect verse 24 to this list?
- This section concludes with a warning to the community in verse 26. How would you say this from a positive point of view?
  - ❏ The writer closes with two spiritual disciplines: prayers of thanksgiving and intercession, and communion. Both assume that one is involved in the community deeply enough to be able to pray on behalf of others as well as to seek the prayers of others and to partake of the Lord's Supper together. How does one reach this point?
  - ❏ What do you see as the place of the community in living in the Spirit?
- Conclude by praying the Great Prayer of Thanksgiving from the liturgy for the Celebration of the Lord's Supper (*Book of Common Worship* [Louisville: Westminster/John Knox Press, 1993], 69).

iBelieve

OPTIONAL ACTIVITIES

- Art charades: Print each fruit of the Spirit on an index card. Have a group member take one card and draw something on newsprint that portrays that fruit of the Spirit. The group is to guess which one is being illustrated.

- Spiritual discipline: Pray intercessory prayers. Begin in silence, then invite anyone who wishes to pray to do so. If the group is not used to doing this, ask first for prayer concerns, then suggest that individuals might pray aloud and silently for these concerns, as well as others on their hearts. Conclude with: "We lift to you, God of all creation, these concerns that we have spoken aloud, as well as those that we speak in the silence of our hearts. Amen."

NOTES:

SMALL-GROUP STUDY
For discussion of Days 29–35 in the daily reader;
to be used after Day 35

$\mathcal{S}$ession 5

Disciplines of the Spirit

FOCUS

Finding ways to work for the good of all.

MAIN IDEAS

Live and let live. Don't bother other people, or expect them to bother you. While a certain wisdom may underlie this approach, in practice it easily slides from tolerance to indifference. In a culture where rugged individualism is prized, these dicta are too easily championed. How do we work for the good of all, nevertheless?

These days it is common for friends and family members to conduct "interventions" when they discover that someone they care about has become addicted to alcohol or another drug. An intervention can always be misunderstood, and thus fail to achieve the objective. In fact, there is always the risk that matters will become worse. Still, people who care deeply about the welfare of another will take the risk for the sake of the other. Paul encouraged the Christians of Galatia to intervene when they saw a fellow believer slipping into some sort of spiritual or moral danger. Yet, one must intervene cautiously and prayerfully, aware of one's own vulnerability. Paul urged "a spirit of gentleness." Is such an intervention conceivable in a contemporary North American congregation?

Those who accept the responsibility of intervening for the sake of a sister or brother must also be willing to welcome one who comes to them with an objective appraisal of their behavior. The goal is mutuality, not that some should have an exclusive right to evaluate the behavior of others.

Two spiritual disciplines that may help us take responsibility for one another are confession and service to the church and the community. Confession and absolution are entirely separate from psychotherapy. Their goal is to heal a spiritual problem rather than a psychological or emotional one. The voice of the other offering

pardon somehow conveys God's voice more effectively. Paul urges the Christians of Galatia not to tire of trying to do the right thing. He promises that, in the end, in God's great and final day, those who have given themselves to "live by the Spirit" will experience a glorious confirmation.

PREPARING TO LEAD
- Explore the meaning and value of confession and absolution or pardon.
    - ❑ We often hear that confession is good for the soul; why is that so?
    - ❑ What is the difference between confessing to God and to a human being? How is confession between Christians different from talking with a professional therapist?
    - ❑ What is the place of the Prayer of Confession in the service of worship?
- Explore the meaning of Galatians 6:2 in a day when violence seems closer to home than ever and many families reside a far distance from other family members.
    - ❑ How is it that we are to bear one another's burdens?
    - ❑ How do you see this verse connected to the fruit of the Spirit? to the works of the flesh?
- Explore ways to help one another "not grow weary in doing what is right" (v. 9).
    - ❑ What are the means of providing support to one another? How might a congregation organize to provide such support?
    - ❑ Some congregations organize their deacons to be prepared to help in specific situations, such as at time of birth, at time of death, or when someone is hospitalized. Others form many types of small groups and use them

to provide support to individuals when special help is needed. What does your congregation do?

❑ What atmosphere is necessary for people to be open to providing such support and for the persons needing it to be open to accepting it?

GATHERING ACTIVITIES
(Use as appropriate.)

- List sayings that Paul turns upside down in Galatians, such as "live and let live."

- Produce steps for bearing one another's burdens, specifically for doing that within your congregation. What programs or plans need to be in place? How might people be informed and encouraged to participate? Write your ideas on newsprint so they can be presented to the appropriate church committees or boards.

GUIDING THE DISCUSSION

- Read Galatians 6:1–10 aloud in at least two translations as in the previous sessions.

- Discuss the three situations presented in "In a Spirit of Gentleness" (Day 34). Apply Galatians 6:1 and Matthew 7:1 to each situation. In summarizing what might be done in each situation, focus on the well-being of the individual and of the community.

- Read Galatians 6:9–10. As you conclude this unit, have the participants name the discussions and disciplines that have been most meaningful to them. Talk together about ways to support one another so that you do not burn out or grow weary.

- Conclude with a time of intercessory prayer, silent and spoken. Do not rush this time; allow time for it as you approach the end of the session.

Optional Activities

- Resource person: We are not always able to break through the facade of a person needing help, and many congregations sponsor counseling services of varying types to speak to others in love and to work for the good of all. If such an agency in your community is church-sponsored, invite a staff member to tell the group about the work done there and of ways that individuals can be a part of this ministry.

- Spiritual discipline: One way to find support and encouragement to keep on going is to develop a relationship with a spiritual friend. Suggest to the group that they might select another person, perhaps in the group, to be a spiritual friend for a period of time. They will keep in touch regularly in person or over the phone, learning the prayer needs of the other person and speaking encouragement and discernment in gentleness. If you think it will work, have the group draw names and try this discipline with another person for a month. Not all the pairings will work, but those that do may become lifelong friends.

Notes: